SPECTRUM

Spelling

Grade 5

Published by
Frank Schaffer Publications®

Frank Schaffer Publications®

Spectrum is an imprint of Frank Schaffer Publications.

Send all inquiries to:
Frank Schaffer Publications
8720 Orion Place
Columbus, Ohio 43240-2111

Spectrum Spelling—grade 5

ISBN 0-7696-5265-4

5 6 HPS 11 10 09

Table of Contents Grade 5

Table of Contents, continued

Pronunciation Key and Sample Words

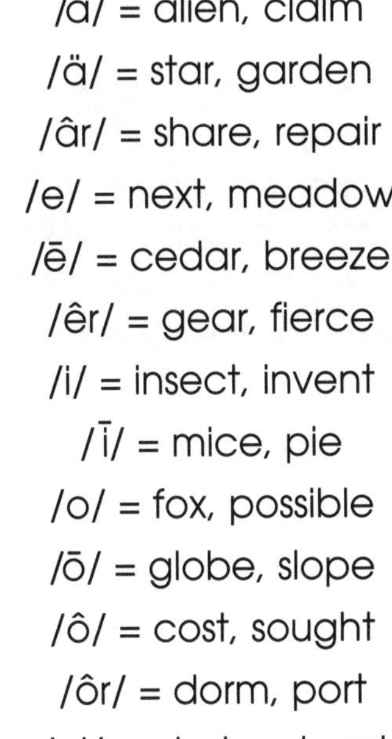

/a/ = and, accident
/ā/ = alien, claim
/ä/ = star, garden
/âr/ = share, repair
/e/ = next, meadow
/ē/ = cedar, breeze
/êr/ = gear, fierce
/i/ = insect, invent
/ī/ = mice, pie
/o/ = fox, possible
/ō/ = globe, slope
/ô/ = cost, sought
/ôr/ = dorm, port
/oi/ = choice, loyal
/ou/ = couch, powder
/u/ = usher, summer
/ū/ = muse, bugle
/ü/ = flute, June
/u̇/ = brook, full
/û/ = courage, journal
/ch/ = beach, channel
/ng/ = hanger, strong
/sh/ = ship, splash
/th/ = three, cloth
/th/ = these, feather
/hw/ = whale, wheat
/zh/ = pleasure, measure
/ə/ = a = about, purchase
e = item, happen
i = habit, pencil
o = other, mother
u = up, crust

NAME ____________________

Lesson 1 Short Vowels: **a**, **e**, **i**

Say each of the following words out loud, stressing the short vowel sounds. Then, write the words on the lines provided.

Spelling Tip

Short **a** can be spelled **a**, short **e** can be spelled **e** and **ea**, and short **i** is spelled **i**. The symbol for short **a** is /a/. The symbol for short **e** is /e/. The symbol for short **i** is /i/.

Spelling Words

perhaps ____________________

necklace ____________________

sweater ____________________

inch ____________________

happen ____________________

empty ____________________

invent ____________________

athlete ____________________

elephant ____________________

until ____________________

accident ____________________

spell ____________________

city ____________________

adventure ____________________

important ____________________

NAME ______________________

Lesson 1 Short Vowels: **a**, **e**, **i**

Challenge

Circle the other words that have a short **a**, **e**, or **i** sound.

Words in Context

Use the spelling words to fill in the missing blanks. Pay careful attention to the spelling as you write each word in the blank.

1. Mitzi wore a pretty bracelet and a beautiful ________________.
2. I am studying about a big, gray ________________ in Africa.
3. The ________________ broke the record for the fastest time.
4. Larry lived in the capital ________________.
5. Sheryl wore a pink ________________ yesterday.
6. Be careful as you drive so you don't have an ________________.
7. Who will ________________ the next space tool?
8. Ann can ________________ the best in the class.
9. ________________ we can go to the movies tomorrow night.
10. It measured an ________________ long.
11. Wait ________________ tomorrow, and we'll go together.
12. Please ________________ the cans before you put them in the bag.
13. What do you think will ________________ at the end of the book?
14. Please sign the ________________ papers on your desk.
15. Our trip was quite an ________________.

Word Building

Compound words are two words joined together that form a new word. Use the following lines to write as many compound words as you can using the word *neck*.

________________ ________________ ________________

________________ ________________ ________________

NAME ______________________________

Lesson 1 Short Vowels: a, e, i

Fun with Words

Find the 15 spelling words with short **a**, **e**, and **i** vowels in the puzzle below. The words can be forward, backward, horizontal, vertical, and diagonal.

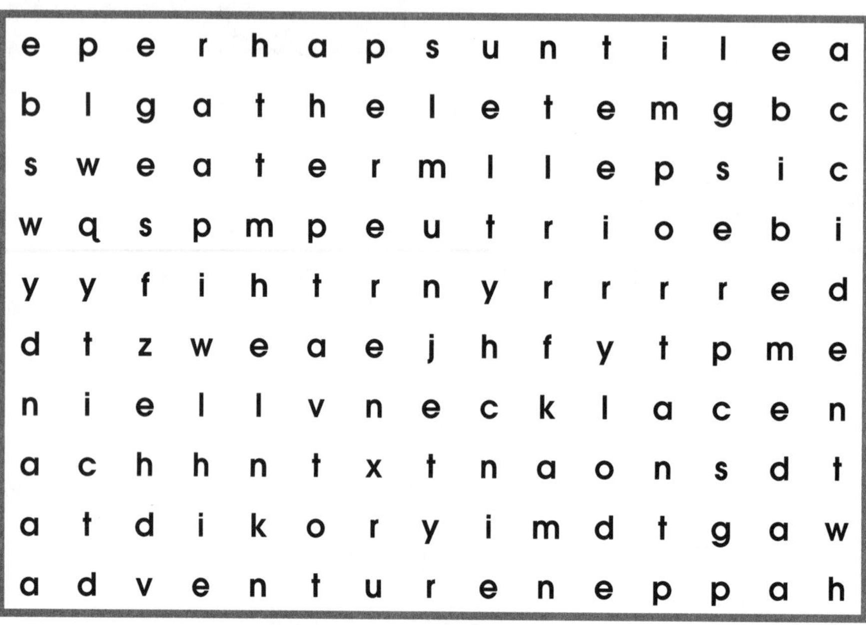

Words Across the Curriculum

Write the geography words on the lines.

1. Africa ____________________

2. nomads ____________________

3. elevations____________________

4. discover ____________________

5. India ____________________

Complete the following paragraph with words from above.

Many people travel the countries to visit and explore. South ____________________ and ____________________ are two countries explored for cultural and historic reasons. Visitors there might learn about ____________________ who lived in the deserts. Many of these people spent their lives crossing their country, sometimes crossing mountains with high ____________________. They were known for their agricultural processes. When traveling, there is much to ______________and learn.

NAME ______________________

Lesson 1 Short Vowels: a, e, i

Words in Writing

Write a paragraph about a nomadic group of people. Use at least five words from the box.

perhaps	inch	invent	until	city	Africa	discover
necklace	happen	athlete	accident	adventure	nomads	India
sweater	empty	elephant	spell	important	elevations	

____

____

____

____

____

____

____

____

____

____

____

Misspelled Words

Read the paragraph below. Circle the misspelled words. Write the correct spelling above the misspelled word.

A nomad is a member of a group of people who do not have a stable home. Nomeds wander from place to place unitil they find food, water, and land to graze their animals. Nomad tribes still live in areas of Africae, Asia, Australia, and the Arctic region. Some nomades have seasonal homes. These groups of people are seminomadic.

NAME ____________________

Lesson 2 Short Vowels: **o, u**

Say each of the following words out loud, stressing the short vowel sounds. Then, write the words on the lines.

Spelling Tip	The short **o** sound can be spelled with **o**, **au**, **aw**, **oa**, or **ough**. These letter patterns can have slightly different sounds for short **o**. The symbols for short **o** are /o/ and /ô/. The short **u** sound is spelled with the letter **u**. The symbol for short **u** is /u/.

Spelling Words

possible ____________________

because ____________________

straw ____________________

broad ____________________

bought ____________________

swung ____________________

problem ____________________

taught ____________________

paw ____________________

sought ____________________

jungle ____________________

brought ____________________

shuttle ____________________

lobster ____________________

umbrella ____________________

NAME ______________________

Lesson 2 Short Vowels: **o, u**

Words in Context
Complete the following dialogue using the spelling words. Not all spelling words are used.

Challenge

Circle the other words that have the short **o** or **u** sound.

Maya had ________________ her special vegetarian pizza for the school cook-off. Now, it looked like Gina had brought the same thing. ________________ it was a contest, students were not supposed to bring the same recipe. This was a ________________. Maya set her pan on the ________________ food table. Then, she ________________ her teacher.

"How is this ________________?" she asked Mrs. Kaye.

"It's not a problem," answered Mrs. Kaye. "How can we change your recipe?" Mrs. Kaye had always ________________ her students to think creatively.

"Hmm...," thought Maya. "I know," she blurted. "But it will take me a few minutes."

Fortunately, Maya was early. She found her mother in the auditorium, who had ________________ extra ingredients. First, they spread the tortilla chips in a bowl shaped like an upside down ________________. Then, they scooped the sauce and vegetables off of the pizza crust and plopped it on the tortilla chips. They sprinkled a little more cheese and added a dab of sour cream. Maya had a new recipe: vegetarian nachos. They were the hit of the cook-off!

NAME ______________________

Lesson 2 Short Vowels: **o, u**

Fun with Words

Look at the following pictures. Next to each picture, write a sentence using one of the spelling words from this lesson. Underline the spelling word in your sentence.

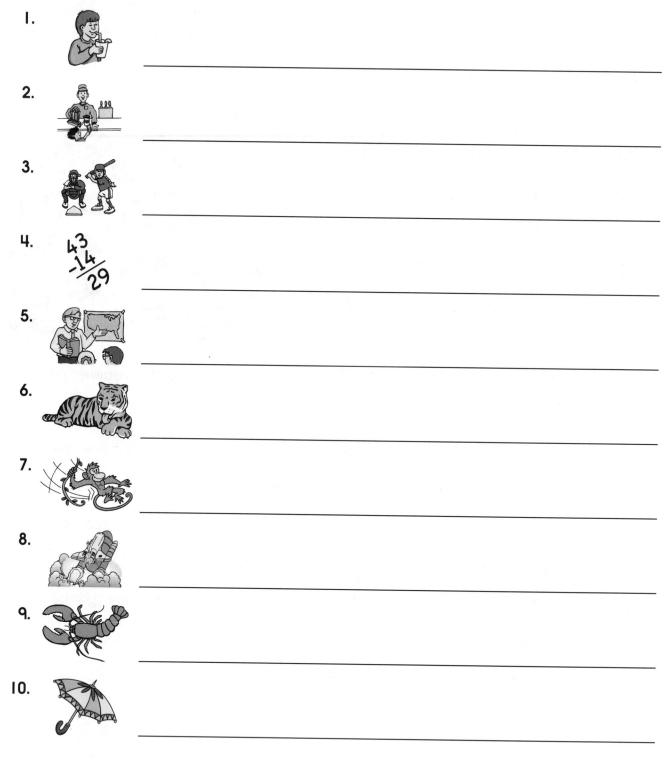

1.  ______________________

2.  ______________________

3.  ______________________

4. 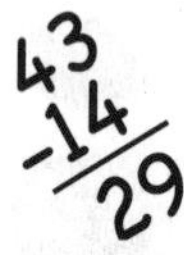

____

5.  ______________________

6.  ______________________

7.  ______________________

8.  ______________________

9.  ______________________

10.  ______________________

NAME ____________________

Lesson 2 Short Vowels: **o, u**

Words in Writing

Write a short passage about your favorite animal. Use at least five words from the box.

____

____

____

____

____

____

____

____

____

____

possible	broad	problem	sought	shuttle
because	bought	taught	jungle	lobster
straw	swung	paw	brought	umbrella

Using the Dictionary

The word you look up in a dictionary is called an **entry word**. Entry words in a dictionary are arranged alphabetically. Put words in the box in alphabetical order.

______	______	______
______	______	______
______	______	______
______	______	______
______	______	______

NAME ____________________

Review Lessons 1–2

LESSONS 1–2 REVIEW

Write each of the following words on the lines. Then, circle the letters that make each word have the short **a** or **i** sound.

1. important ____________
2. adventure ____________
3. city ____________
4. accident ____________
5. until ____________
6. athlete ____________
7. invent ____________
8. and ____________
9. inch ____________
10. nomads ____________

Write a spelling word that has the short **e** sound that completes each of the following sentences. Then, circle the letter or letters that make this word have the short **e** sound.

1. I can ____________ all of the words from this list correctly.
2. The ____________ is being moved to an animal sanctuary in Tennessee.
3. I was hungry and the box of cereal was ____________.
4. My sister wants a new ____________ to wear on her birthday.
5. My father got me a sparkling ____________ to wear on my birthday.

NAME ________________________

Review Lessons 1–2

Complete the following paragraph with the spelling words from the box that have the short **o** sound. Then, circle the letter or letters that give the words the short **o** sound.

because	paw	problem	taught
brought	possible	sought	

Henry had a puppy. But the puppy had a ________________ with his ________________. The puppy was Henry's pet and best friend. Henry needed to take care of the puppy ________________ he was the guardian. Henry's teacher had ________________ his class a lesson on veterinarians. Maybe it was ________________ he could take his puppy to a vet. He ________________ out the office on Wilkson Street with his parents and took his puppy there. The doctor said she was glad Henry ________________ his puppy to the vet. She could make him well again.

Complete the following sentences with spelling words in the box that have the short **u** sound.

jungle	shuttle	swung	umbrella

1. Monkeys live in the ________________.
2. The children ________________ on the swing set in the park.
3. The students liked learning about the space ________________ in school.
4. Take an ________________; it looks like it will rain.

LESSONS 1–2 REVIEW

NAME ____________________

Lesson 3 Long Vowels: **a**, **e**, **i**

Say each of the following words out loud, stressing the long vowel sounds. Then, write the words on the lines provided.

Spelling Tip	Long **a** can be spelled **a**, **ai**, **ay**, **ea**, **eigh**, and **a-consonant-e**. The symbol for long **a** is /ā/. Long **e** can be spelled **ea**, **ee**, **ei**, **ie**, and **y**. The symbol for long **e** is /ē/. Long **i** can be spelled **i**, **igh**, **y**, and **i-consonent-e**. The symbol for long **i** is /ī/.

Spelling Words

vacation ____________________

reach ____________________

describe ____________________

sustain ____________________

sleep ____________________

flight ____________________

break ____________________

seize ____________________

sky ____________________

weigh ____________________

field ____________________

pioneer ____________________

airplane ____________________

study ____________________

clay ____________________

NAME ___________________________

Lesson 3 Long Vowels: **a, e, i**

Words in Context

Complete the following paragraph using the spelling words. Not every spelling word is used.

Wilbur and Orville Wright

How would you ________________ a ________________? A pioneer is not just a person who crossed a corn ________________ of America in the old west. A pioneer is someone who opens the way for others. Who opened the way to the ________________? The Wright brothers did. Orville and Wilbur Wright were born in Dayton, Ohio in the mid-1800s. In 1903, near Kitty Hawk, North Carolina, the Wright brothers made the first sustained ________________ in a power-driven ________________. The Wright brothers continued to ________________ several flying records. A great ________________ would be to visit the Wright Brothers National Memorial in Kill Devil Hills, North Carolina.

Word Building

The spelling words below are verbs. Regular present tense verbs are made into past tense by adding **ed**. Write the four spelling words on the lines. Then, write the past tense form of these verbs on the lines beside them. If a verb ends in the letter **y**, change the **y** to **i** and then add **ed**.

reach ________________ ________________

seize ________________ ________________

weigh ________________ ________________

study ________________ ________________

NAME ______________________

Lesson 3 Long Vowels: a, e, i

Fun with Words

Create a word pyramid. The bottom layer of the pyramid is built with spelling words with the long **a** sound. The next layer up is built with long **e** spelling words. The third layer is built with long **i** spelling words. The top three layers are built with long **a**, **e**, and **i** words of your choice.

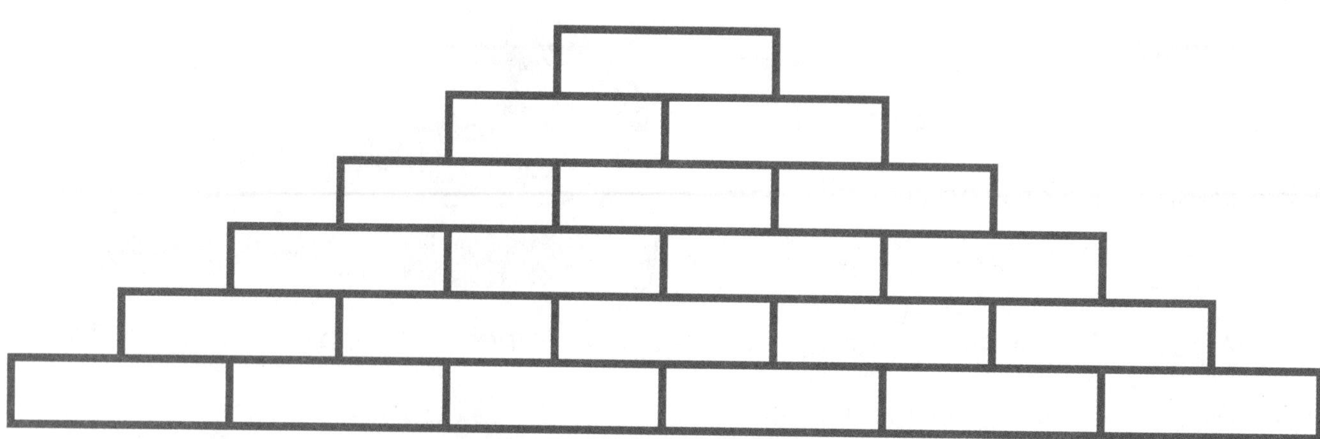

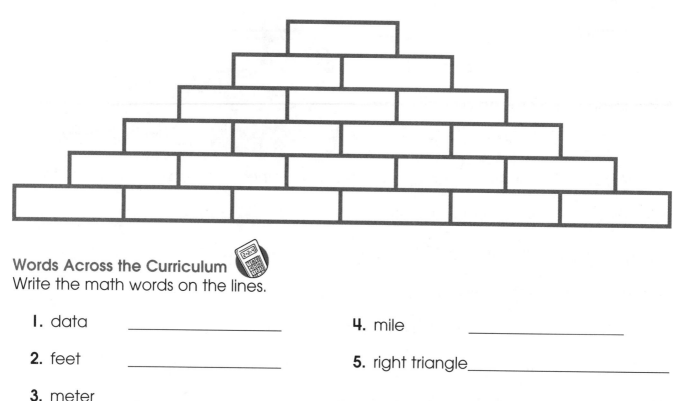

Words Across the Curriculum

Write the math words on the lines.

1. data ______________
2. feet ______________
3. meter ______________
4. mile ______________
5. right triangle ______________

Read each definition below, then write the word next to its definition. Use a dictionary if you need help.

1. ______________: a standard measure of length, equal to 5,280 feet or 1,760 yards or 1.6093 kilometers
2. ______________: plural of foot; a unit of length equal to 12 inches or 0.3048 meter
3. ______________: a triangle with a 90° angle
4. ______________: facts or figures which can be studied in order to make conclusions or judgments
5. ______________: a unit of measure that is the basic unit in the metric system; it is equal to 39.37 inches

NAME ______________________

Lesson 3 Long Vowels: **a, e, i**

Words in Writing

Interview a teacher in your school who knows a lot about math. Use at least five words from the box to write a paragraph of your conversation.

vacation	**sustain**	**break**	**weigh**	**airplane**	**data**	**mile**
reach	**sleep**	**seize**	**field**	**study**	**feet**	**right**
describe	**flight**	**sky**	**pioneer**	**clay**	**meter**	**triangle**

____

____

____

____

____

____

____

Misspelled Words

Have you heard the Latin expression *carpe diem*? You have probably heard it translated to English: *Seize the Day!* This expression means *to enjoy the day and all of its opportunities* and *to live for the moment.* Proofread the following ways you may seize the day. Write the correct spelling above the misspelled words, using proofreading marks.

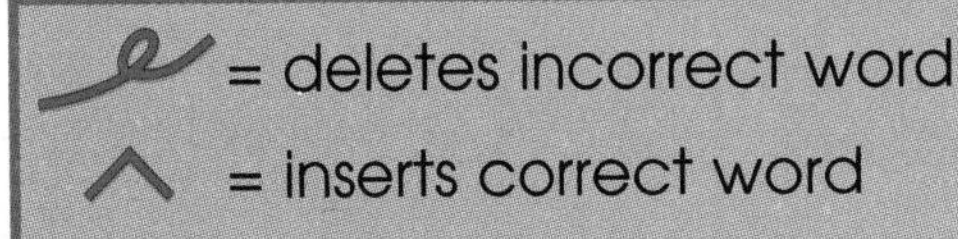

1. take a long vaycation
2. braik a record in a 5K race
3. learn to fly an airpleighn
4. pioneir a new invention
5. run barefoot through a fieeld
6. studie a new language
7. observe birds in flite
8. fly a glider through the skigh
9. create pottery with clae
10. seaze the day

NAME ______________________

Lesson 4 Long Vowels: **o, u**

Say each of the following words out loud, stressing the long vowel sounds. Then, write the words on the lines provided. Over emphasize the difference between the /ū/ and the /ü/.

Spelling Tip

Long **o** can be spelled **o, oa, ow,** and **o-consonant-e**. The symbol for long **o** is /ō/. Long **u** has two sounds. The /ū/ sound can be spelled **u** and has a /y/ sound at the beginning of the vowel. The /ü/ sound can be spelled **u, ue, ew, oo, ou, u-consonant-e,** and **ui-consonant-e**. The difference between /ū/ and /ü/ is slight.

Spelling Words

bogus ______________________

uniform ______________________

coach ______________________

truth ______________________

bowl ______________________

true ______________________

antelope ______________________

crew ______________________

school ______________________

group ______________________

parachute ______________________

bruise ______________________

future ______________________

ooze ______________________

reduce ______________________

NAME ______________________

Lesson 4 Long Vowels: **o, u**

Words in Context

Complete the following sentences using spelling words

1. Monica liked her new band ________________.
2. There was red ________________ coming out of Mark's volcano science experiment.
3. The soccer ________________ announced that practice would begin right after school.
4. The ________________ is yet to be known.
5. Jerry likes a big ________________ of cereal for breakfast.
6. Kyoko got a ________________ on her knee when she fell off of her bike.
7. The ________________ opened right on time.
8. The ________________ is related to the oxen and the goat.
9. The whole ________________ of students enjoyed the field trip.
10. The ________________ of the space shuttle was excited for the trip.
11. Abraham participated in many ________________ activities.
12. The teacher asked a series of ________________ or false questions.
13. Don't spend the monopoly money; it is ________________ money.
14. I will not lie; I will always tell the ________________.
15. Put ice on your bruised knee to help ________________ the swelling.

NAME ______________________

Lesson 4 Long Vowels: **o, u**

Fun with Words

Read the following sentences. After each question, write whether the sentence is **true** or **false**. Then, circle the spelling word or words found in the sentence.

1. A parachute is used to slow down a person dropping from an airplane. ______________
2. You wouldn't find a coach in a school. ______________
3. Antelope are related to oxen and goats. ______________
4. If you drop an apple, it might bruise. ______________
5. If you reduce the number in a group, then you will have more. ______________
6. One might find ooze on the trunk of a maple tree. ______________
7. A one-man team is called a *crew*. ______________
8. The future is a time in the past. ______________

Words Across the Curriculum

Write the following science words on the lines.

1. fuse ______________
2. molecule ______________
3. nuclear ______________
4. nucleus ______________
5. proton ______________

Write the science word next to its definition. Use a dictionary if you need help.

1. ______________: This particle has a single, electric charge. It is part of the nucleus of an atom.
2. ______________: The verb form of this word means *to unite* or to *join together by melting*.
3. ______________: This is the center part of the atom.
4. ______________: This adjective involves the use of the nuclei of atoms.
5. ______________: This is the smallest particle of a substance that can exist alone without losing its chemical form.

NAME ______________________________

Lesson 4 Long Vowels: o, u

Words in Writing

Write a letter to a friend using at least five spelling words.

____

____

____

____

____

____

____

Using the Dictionary

The sound difference between the /ü/ and the /ū/ spellings can seem quite slight. However, when you pronounce the words, you can hear a difference. The vowel sounds in the following pronunciations are missing. Add the correct symbol for the sound. Then, write the word.

/ü/ = ōō
/ū/ = yōō

1. br___z ______________
2. kr___ ______________
3. f_____′ chər ______________
4. gr___p ______________
5. ___z ______________
6. per′ ə sh___t ______________
7. rē d___s′ ______________
8. sk___l ______________
9. tr___ ______________
10. tr___th ______________
11. _______n′ ə fôrm ______________
12. f_______z ______________
13. mäl′ ə k_______l ______________
14. n___′ klē ər ______________
15. n___′ klē əs ______________

NAME ____________________

Review Lessons 3–4

Write each of the spelling words below. Then, circle the letter or letters that make each word have the long **a**, **e**, or **i** sound.

1. sustain ______________
2. way ______________
3. break ______________
4. weigh ______________
5. reach ______________
6. pioneer ______________
7. seize ______________
8. field ______________
9. flight ______________
10. sky ______________

LESSONS 3–4 REVIEW

Write a word from Lesson 3 that has the long **a**, **e**, or **i** sound that completes each of the following sentences.

1. Are you going to take a ______________ this spring break?
2. Melissa is hoping to ______________ the long jump record.
3. The ______________ is delayed and won't arrive for another hour.
4. Michael found out his great-great-grandmother was a ______________.
5. Leigh and Bob love to ______________ mountains.
6. The ______________ is really blue today.
7. The trucks have to pass through the ______________ stations on the freeway.
8. The lost and found officer asked Sandra to ______________ the missing bracelet.
9. The farmers plowed the ______________ and prepared for the following day's work.
10. The birds' ______________ patterns are amazing to watch.

NAME ____________________

Review Lessons 3–4

Write each of the following spelling words. Then, circle the letter or letters that make each word have the long **o** or long **u** sound.

1. coach ____________
2. bowl ____________
3. antelope ____________
4. uniform ____________
5. true ____________
6. crew ____________
7. school ____________
8. group ____________
9. parachute ____________
10. bruise ____________

Complete the following paragraph with the spelling words from Lesson 4 that have the long **o** or **u** sound. Then, circle other words in the paragraph with a long **o** or **u** sound.

The team was ready. It was a beautiful day. The members of the ____________ had been practicing for months and in all types of weather. The ____________ was proud of her team. It was a slow start. Many girls dropped out. The ____________ weren't ready for the first meet. One girl suffered a serious ____________ and had to take several weeks off. The weather wasn't cooperating either. But now, the ____________ was in the semifinals. One more regatta, or boat race, and the ____________ would advance to the finals. Today was this team's day. Today, the ____________ would be known. They were ready!

LESSONS 3–4 REVIEW

NAME ______________________

Lesson 5 Variant Consonants: **j, k**

Say the following words out loud. Then, write each one on the lines provided.

Spelling Tip	The /j/ sound can be spelled with **j** or **g**. The /k/ sound can be spelled with **k**, **c**, or **ch**.

Spelling Words

banjo ______________________

broken ______________________

general ______________________

American ______________________

major ______________________

kitten ______________________

ginger ______________________

camp ______________________

object ______________________

market ______________________

legend ______________________

character ______________________

subject ______________________

monkey ______________________

electric ______________________

NAME ______________________

Lesson 5 Variant Consonants: j, k

Words in Context

Use spelling words to complete the paragraph. Not every word is used.

Challenge

Circle other words with the /j/ and /k/ sounds.

Sullivan Ballou

Have you ever heard of Major Sullivan Ballou? He may not be a famous ________________ of the ________________ Civil War, but he should definitely be remembered. Ballou was a strong supporter of President Abraham Lincoln. He decided to enlist in the Union Army and serve under ________________ Ulysses S. Grant. ________________ Sullivan Ballou was stationed at Camp Clark, a ________________ near Washington, D.C. Ballou did not have a good feeling about the upcoming battle. Though his spirits were not ________________, he did not believe he would survive the war. At Camp Clark, he wrote a letter to his wife. The ________________ was his love for her and their children, his passion for the Union Army, and his worries about dying in battle. Fifteen days later, at the First Battle of Bull Run, Major Ballou and many of his men were killed. Altogether, four thousand Americans lost their lives at this battle. Major Ballou's letter is now published. You can learn more about this brave soldier with remarkable ________________ by reading his letter.

Word Building

Synonyms are words that have the same or similar meaning. Write the spelling word that is a synonym of each word below.

1. famous ________________
2. dynamic ________________
3. item ________________
4. shattered ________________
5. shelter ________________
6. store ________________

NAME ______________________

Lesson 5 Variant Consonants: **j, k**

Fun with Words

Complete the puzzle using spelling words.

Across

1. The ______ light went out during the storm.
3. You can pick up fruit and vegetables at the ______.
5. A ______ is a stringed musical instrument.
7. The ______ of the game *Jeopardy* is to provide the questions to given answers.

Down

2. You can adopt a dog, puppy, cat, or ______, from an animal shelter.
3. A ______ lives in a jungle.
4. Social studies is one ______ in school.
6. ______ is a spice made from the root of a plant.

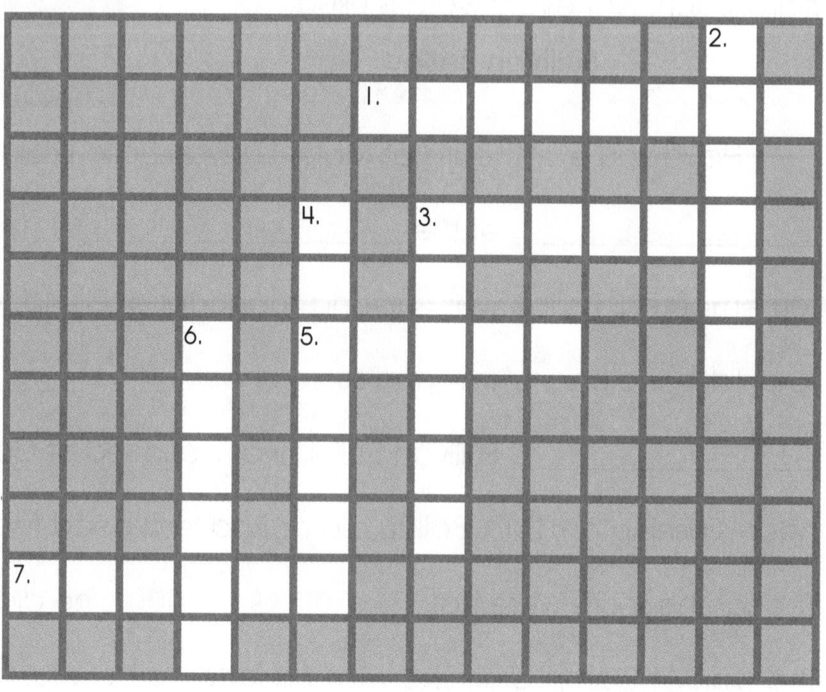

Words Across the Curriculum

Write the social studies words on the lines.

1. captain ______________
2. climate ______________
3. crew ______________
4. geography ______________
5. voyage ______________

Complete the following sentences with social studies words.

1. ______________ James Cook was an explorer who commanded the ship, *Endeavor.*
2. He and his ______________ set sail in 1768.
3. Their ______________ circumnavigated the globe.
4. On his second trip, he explored the cold ______________ of the Antarctic Ocean.
5. During his third trip, Cook tested his knowledge of ______________ to find the Northwest passage.

NAME ____________________

Lesson 5 Variant Consonants: j, k

Words in Writing

Write a biography about a famous figure from history. Use at least five words from the box.

banjo	American	ginger	market	subject	captain	geography
broken	major	camp	legend	monkey	climate	voyage
general	kitten	object	character	electric	crew	

____

____

____

____

____

Misspelled Words

Circle the misspelled words in each sentence and rewrite them correctly.

1. Stacy played her bango all evening. ____________
2. The jeneral was respected by his troops. ____________
3. Thomas played a magor role in winning the baseball game. ____________
4. I like to sprinkle ginjer on my vanilla pudding. ____________
5. Bill loves to go to summer kamp. ____________
6. Mom goes to the marcet every Saturday morning. ____________
7. I have to think of one more charakter for the skit I'm writing. ____________
8. Jane Goodall was given a toy moncey when she was a little girl. ____________
9. Doug will be the kaptain of our football team. ____________
10. I prefer a warmer klimate. ____________

NAME ______________________

Lesson 6 Consonants Digraphs: **ch, ph, sh, th, wh, tch**

Say each word out loud. Then, write each word.

Spelling Tip	**Consonant digraphs** are two or more consonant letters that together make one specific sound.

Spelling Words

chestnut ______________________

trophy ______________________

shutter ______________________

thorn ______________________

pitch ______________________

whale ______________________

chipmunk ______________________

phone ______________________

toothbrush ______________________

month ______________________

patch ______________________

whistle ______________________

speech ______________________

width ______________________

watch ______________________

NAME ______________________________

Lesson 6 Consonants Digraphs: **ch, ph, sh, th, wh, tch**

Words in Context

Complete the following story with spelling words.

It had been three hours since I had received the ______________ call. Mom had asked that I ______________ the tea kettle and turn it off when it began to ______________. I was putting away my ______________ when the water began to boil in the kettle. I turned it off and turned around just as the phone rang. I answered, and the woman on the other end said, "It's time."

I had a ______________ ready for just this occasion, but all I could do was squeak like a little ______________. I asked her when I needed to be ready, figuring it would be a week or a ______________. "Three hours," she replied.

I quickly hung up the phone, ran the ______________ of the room to get my stuff, closed the ______________ on the front window, and locked the front door behind me. Mom was working in the garden when I told her where I was going. That was three hours ago.

The ______________ trees swayed in the wind. A cloud as big as a ______________ floated above me. I stood on a ______________ of dirt in the center of the field. I still couldn't believe I was called up to ______________. I was nervous when I threw the first pitch. It felt like a ______________ was poking me. But after nine innings, I brought home a ______________ from my first little league baseball start.

NAME ______________________

Lesson 6 Consonants Digraphs: **ch, ph, sh, th, wh, tch**

Fun with Words

Look at the following pictures. Next to each picture, write a sentence using the spelling word that names the picture. Underline the spelling word in your sentence.

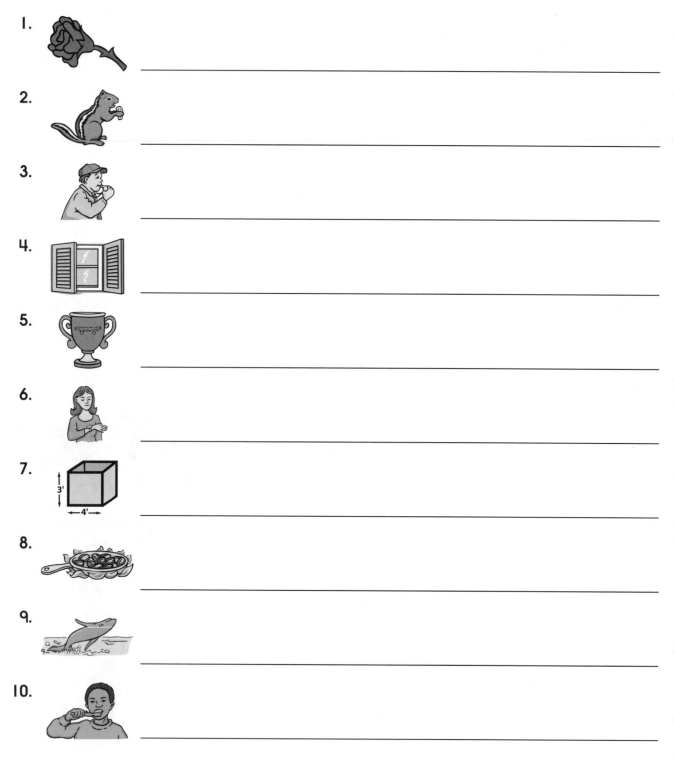

1.  ______________________

2.  ______________________

3.  ______________________

4.  ______________________

5.  ______________________

6.  ______________________

7. 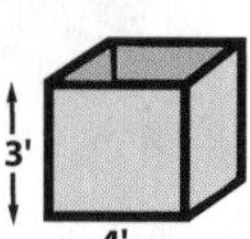

____

8.  ______________________

9.  ______________________

10.  ______________________

NAME ______________________

Lesson 6 Consonants Digraphs: **ch, ph, sh, th, wh, tch**

Words in Writing

Write a fictional dialogue between at least three characters about a sporting event. Use at least five words from the box.

chestnut	thorn	chipmunk	month	speech
trophy	pitch	phone	patch	width
shutter	whale	toothbrush	whistle	watch

____

____

____

____

____

____

____

Using the Dictionary

Look up each spelling word in a dictionary and write the parts of speech listed.

1. chestnut ______________
2. trophy ______________
3. shutter ______________
4. thorn ______________
5. pitch ______________
6. whale ______________
7. chipmunk ______________
8. phone ______________
9. toothbrush ______________
10. month ______________
11. patch ______________
12. whistle ______________
13. speech ______________
14. width ______________
15. watch ______________

NAME ______________________

Lesson 7 Consonant Blends: **bl, fl, br, cr, gr, sk, sp, st**

Say each word out loud. Then, write each word on the lines provided.

Spelling Tip	**Consonant blends** are two or more consonant letters that run together. Each letter is still heard.

Spelling Words

blend ______________________

conflict ______________________

branch ______________________

cream ______________________

grant ______________________

risk ______________________

respect ______________________

frost ______________________

bloom ______________________

flash ______________________

breakfast ______________________

secret ______________________

grade ______________________

skunk ______________________

spinach ______________________

NAME ____________________

Lesson 7 Consonant Blends: **bl, fl, br, cr, gr, sk, sp, st**

Words in Context

Complete each sentence with spelling words.

1. ______________ is a very good food for you to eat.
2. Don't forget to ______________ the strawberries and bananas together.
3. I think I see and smell a ______________ over in the trees.
4. The class had a ______________ over which book to read.
5. The teacher will ______________ the papers this weekend.
6. The tree ______________ looks small compared to the big tree.
7. Stacy promised not to tell her best friend's ______________.
8. Do you like ______________ in your coffee?
9. Grace likes pancakes with syrup for ______________.
10. The teacher said she would ______________ a reading request from each student.
11. The lightning was like a ______________ in the sky.
12. Bridget took a ______________ and attempted to run the whole distance.
13. The flowers will ______________ in the spring.
14. The students had a lot of ______________ for their teacher.
15. The ______________ came early this fall.

Word Building

Antonyms are words that have the opposite or close to the opposite meanings of each other. Write the spelling words that are the antonyms of the words below.

1. separate ______________
2. agreement ______________
3. refuse ______________
4. safe ______________
5. scorn ______________

NAME ______________________

Lesson 7 Consonant Blends: **bl, fl, br, cr, gr, sk, sp, st**

Words Across the Curriculum

Write the health words on the lines.

1. cerebrum ______________
2. spleen ______________
3. stomach ______________

Use a dictionary to write a brief description of each of these parts of the body. Then, match the part to the illustration. Write the name of the body part next to the appropriate illustration.

1. ____

____

2. ____

____

3. ____

____

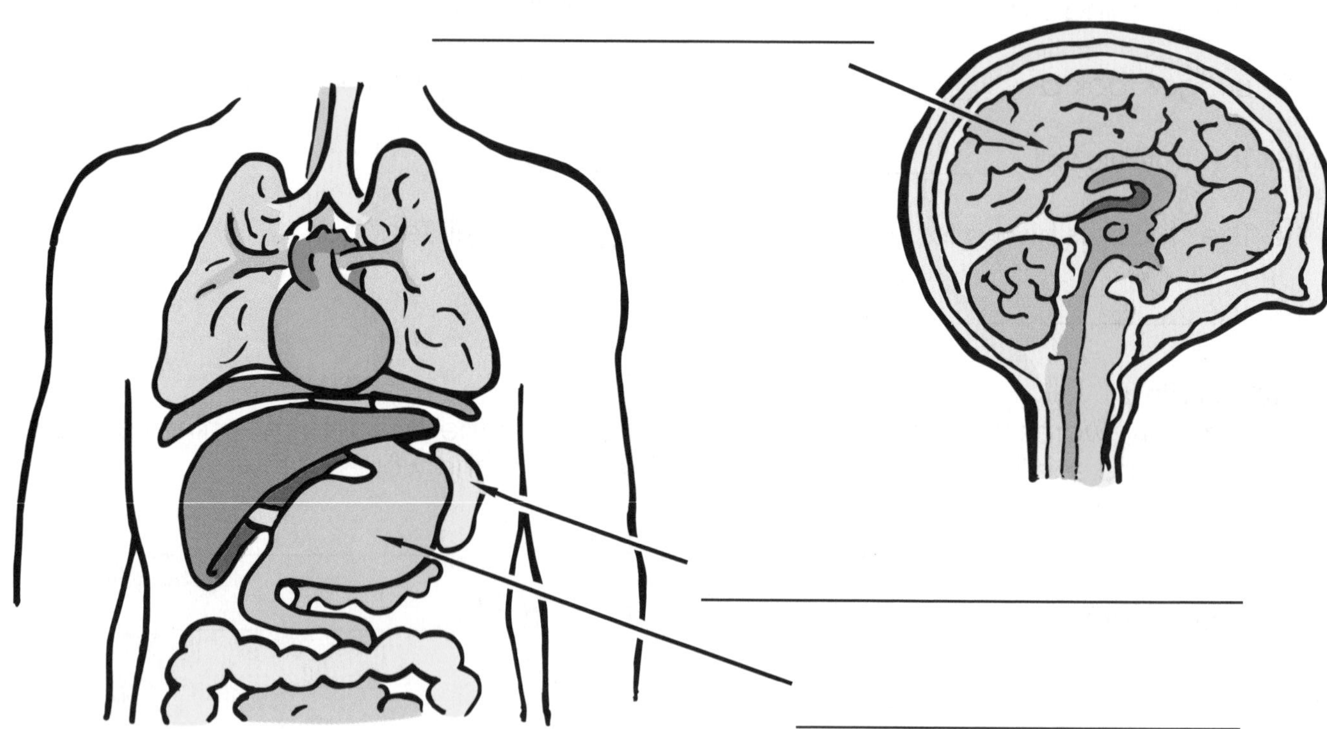

NAME ______________________________

Lesson 7 Consonant Blends: bl, fl, br, cr, gr, sk, sp, st

Words in Writing

Write a short story or poem about someone you respect. Use at least five words from the box.

blend	**cream**	**respect**	**flash**	**grade**	**cerebrum**
conflict	**grant**	**frost**	**breakfast**	**skunk**	**spleen**
branch	**risk**	**bloom**	**secret**	**spinach**	**stomach**

____

____

____

____

____

Misspelled Words

Use the proofreading symbols to correct misspellings in the recipe below. If you try this recipe at home, be sure you have adult supervision and permission.

Tomato and Spinach Omelet

ℓ	= deletes letters and words
^	= inserts letters and words

- 2 extra large, graid A, cage-free eggs
- I tablespoon heavy creem
- I ounce fresh cooked and drained supinach
- one fresh diced tomato
- salt and pepper to taste
- I teaspoon butter

Preheat skillet on medium heat. Coat pan with extra virgin olive oil.

Belend eggs and creme in bowl. Pour into skillet. Add sphinach and tomatoes to one side of the omelet and sprinkle in pepper and salt. Cook until eggs are solid and thoroughly cooked. Flip egg-only side over the spinach and tomato side. Cook for one or two minutes more, flipping carefully a couple of times. Slide onto plate and serve.

NAME ____________________

Lesson 8 Silent Letters: kn, mb, wr

Say each word out loud. Then, write each word on the line.

Spelling Tip Some consonant combinations produce silent letters. In the consonant combination **kn**, only the **n** is pronounced. In **mb**, only the **m** is pronounced, and in **wr**, only the **r** is pronounced.

Spelling Words

knapsack ____________________

rewrite ____________________

knead ____________________

climber ____________________

wreath ____________________

knee ____________________

wren ____________________

knock ____________________

numb ____________________

wrestle ____________________

knot ____________________

wrist ____________________

know ____________________

plumber ____________________

wrong ____________________

NAME ____________________

Lesson 8 Silent Letters: **kn, mb, wr**

Words in Context

Complete the following paragraph with spelling words. Not every word will be used.

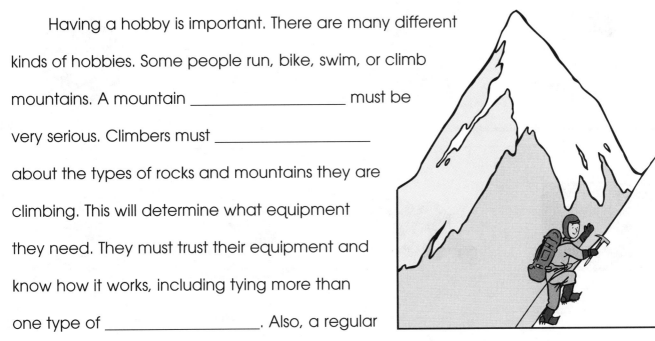

Having a hobby is important. There are many different kinds of hobbies. Some people run, bike, swim, or climb mountains. A mountain ____________ must be very serious. Climbers must ____________ about the types of rocks and mountains they are climbing. This will determine what equipment they need. They must trust their equipment and know how it works, including tying more than one type of ____________. Also, a regular ____________ won't be able to hold all the equipment a climber needs. Climbers must be careful when climbing. If they are not careful, they can hurt a ____________, ____________, or other part of their body.

Climbers must know the weather conditions. It can be very dangerous to be caught on a mountain during bad weather. A ____________ prediction can lead to bad consequences. In extremely cold weather, fingers and toes can become ____________ and hard to move. Climbing is definitely serious business. But most climbers love it and are devoted to spending the time in training and practice to be able to accomplish their goals and enjoy the views from the top of the world.

NAME ________________________

Lesson 8 Silent Letters: **kn, mb, wr**

Fun with Words

Write the spelling word that each picture represents.

1.  ________________

3.  ________________

5.  ________________

7.  ________________

2.  ________________

4.  ________________

6.  ________________

8.  ________________

Words Across the Curriculum

Write the social studies words on the lines below.

1. knights ________________ **3.** wrap ________________

2. tombs ________________

Complete the following paragraph with words from above.

Mummies of the World

Ancient Egyptians would ________________ mummies with cloths in hidden ________________. Native Americans of North America mummified their dead and kept them in caves. The dryness of the caves preserved the bodies. Canadian mummies have been found naturally frozen in glaciers. Kings and ________________ were mummified before being buried in certain parts of Europe. The oldest mummies of the world have been found in South America.

NAME ___________________________

Lesson 8 Silent Letters: **kn, mb, wr**

Words in Writing

Write a paragraph describing your favorite hobby. Include at least five words from the box.

knapsack	climber	wren	wrestle	know	knights
rewrite	wreath	knock	knot	plumber	tombs
knead	knee	numb	wrist	wrong	wrap

____

____

____

____

____

____

Using the Dictionary

Look up the pronunciations of the following spelling words and write them on the lines provided. Notice that the **k** in **kn** words, the **b** in **mb** words, and the **w** in **wr** words are not given in the pronunciation, since they are silent.

1. knapsack ______________
2. rewrite ______________
3. knead ______________
4. climber ______________
5. wreath ______________
6. knee ______________
7. wren ______________
8. knock ______________
9. numb ______________
10. wrestle ______________
11. knot ______________
12. wrist ______________
13. know ______________
14. plumber ______________
15. wrong ______________
16. knights ______________
17. tombs ______________
18. wrap ______________

NAME ______________________

Review Lessons 5–8

Write each of the following words. Circle the consonant sounds /j/ and /k/. Underline the consonant digraphs.

1. banjo ______________
2. monkey ______________
3. watch ______________
4. electric ______________
5. thorn ______________
6. trophy ______________
7. general ______________
8. toothbrush ______________
9. whale ______________
10. chipmunk ______________

Write a word from Lesson 5 or 6 that completes each of the following sentences.

1. My sister is going to ______________ in communication in college.
2. Anna's favorite cookies are ______________ snaps.
3. Jill adopted a ______________ from the humane society.
4. Sam is my favorite ______________ in *The Lord of the Rings.*
5. Donna is going to give a ______________ in her political science class.
6. A cell ______________ can come in very handy in emergencies.
7. The ______________ made a loud noise when the wind blew it closed.
8. Be sure to measure both the height and the ______________ of the box before shipping.
9. The coach blows his ______________ when he is ready to start practice.
10. Who is going to throw the first ______________ at the game?

NAME ____________________

Review Lessons 5–8

Write each of the following words. Circle the consonant blends. Underline the silent letter combinations.

1. blend ____________
2. flash ____________
3. branch ____________
4. cream ____________
5. grant ____________
6. wrestle ____________
7. skunk ____________
8. respect ____________
9. frost ____________
10. knead ____________
11. climber ____________
12. breakfast ____________

Complete the following sentences by filling in the blanks with words from Lesson 7 or 8.

1. A ____________ is a small songbird with a narrow bill and a stubby tail that tilts up.
2. A good morning ____________ for these birds would be insects and fruit.
3. The ____________ of these birds can be quick and irregular.
4. These birds can use their slender bills to investigate a ____________.
5. They nest in cavities, like birdhouses and nests built out of a tree ____________ and grass.
6. A ____________ on a door has become the home of some nests.
7. If you ____________ the sound these songbirds make in your area, you might be able to identify them.

LESSONS 5–8 REVIEW

NAME ______________________

Lesson 9 Vowel Combinations: /al/, /au/, /aw/, /ou/, /oy/, final /əl/

Say each word out loud. Then, write each word on the lines provided.

Spelling Tip

Some vowel combinations make special sounds. The /al/, /au/, and /aw/ sounds make the short **o** sound, as in the word *dog*. It is a slightly longer sound than some other short **o** words. The /ou/ and /oy/ sounds make the vowel sound in *shower*. **Dipthongs** are vowel combinations that make a new sound. The /au/, /aw/, /ou/, /oy/ sounds are dipthongs. The schwa sound is an unaccented vowel followed by an **l** (or other consonant).

Spelling Words

chalk ______________________

August ______________________

crawl ______________________

foundation ______________________

annoy ______________________

cancel ______________________

false ______________________

author ______________________

lawn ______________________

our ______________________

loyal ______________________

label ______________________

salt ______________________

autograph ______________________

outside ______________________

NAME ______________________

Lesson 9 Vowel Combinations: /al/, /au/, /aw/, /ou/, /oy/, final /əl/

Words in Context

Write a spelling word to complete the following sentences.

1. The movie star signed an ______________ as he left the theater.
2. After all of the rain, the ______________ looked nice and green.
3. Since it stopped raining, the students played ______________ during recess.
4. The best friends had been ______________ to each other for years.
5. The teacher used different colored ______________ to write the assignment on the board.
6. The coaches might have to ______________ the game if it doesn't stop raining soon.
7. The ______________ raises money for patients in the hospital.
8. Our teacher said to put a ______________ on our books so they won't get mixed up.
9. The baby is learning to ______________ across the floor.
10. The ______________ has written many good books.

Word Building

Compound words are two words joined together to form a new word. Find the spelling word that is a compound word. Write the word and then write the individual words that are joined together.

Compound Word	Individual Word	Individual Word
1. ______________	______________	______________

The following spelling words can be part of compound words if another word is added. Use a dictionary if you need help.

2. chalk ______________   3. salt ______________

NAME ______________________

Lesson 9 Vowel Combinations: /al/, /au/, /aw/, /ou/, /oy/, final /əl/

Fun with Words

Unscramble the spelling words in the following sentences.

1. The magazine publisher said, "We are yolal ____________ to our ouraht ____________ even though he sometimes will nonya ____________ the readers."
2. The chef said, "If you add tlas ____________ to the sauce, it will alter the flavor."
3. The weather reporter said, "It was a lfesa ____________ report that the storm struck in gsuutA ____________."
4. The mother said, "We are so proud, because rou ____________ baby can waclr ____________ across the entire waln ____________."
5. The director said, "The onainfudaot ____________ must nclace ____________ the event in guAstu ____________ and move it to September."

Words Across the Curriculum

Write the social studies words on the lines.

1. autumn ____________
2. cauliflower ____________
3. drought ____________
4. thaw ____________
5. walnuts ____________

Write the social studies words to complete the paragraph.

If you plan on growing either cauliflower or ____________ there are a few things you should know. Both cauliflower and walnuts need plenty of water. Do not plan on a good crop if you are expecting a ____________. Both ____________ and walnuts are harvested in the ____________. You can eat them fresh in September. If you want to save them, though, you can. You can freeze them and then ____________ them when you are ready to eat them.

NAME ____________________

Lesson 9 Vowel Combinations: /al/, /au/, /aw/, /ou/, /oy/, final /əl/

Words in Writing

Choose ten spelling words and two Words Across the Curriculum words. Write a sentence using each word.

1. ____________________
2. ____________________
3. ____________________
4. ____________________
5. ____________________
6. ____________________
7. ____________________
8. ____________________
9. ____________________
10. ____________________
11. ____________________
12. ____________________

Misspelled Words

Circle the correct answer in each sentence.

1. Please taste the soup before adding (salt, sault) or pepper.
2. After the rain, the (lawn, laun) was green and thick.
3. The sports hero loved to sign her (awtograph, autograph) for her fans.
4. The students were (loyal, loual) to their teacher.
5. The peridot is the birthstone for the month of (Awgust, August).

NAME ______________________

Lesson 10 r-Controlled Vowels: **ar, er, ir, or, ur**

Say each of the following words out loud. Then, write each word on the lines provided.

Spelling Tip

The vowels **a**, **e**, **i**, **o**, and **u** can all be influenced by the letter **r** following them. Words with a **vowel-plus-r** spelling can make their own single-syllable sounds, with the **r** sound emphasized more than the vowel. There are many different symbols for **r**-controlled vowels: /är/ (as in *car*), /er/ (as in *fair*), /ir/ (as in *deer*), /ôr/ (as in *forest*), /ur/ (as in *urban*), and /ər/ for unstressed **r**-controlled vowels.

Spelling Words

apartment ______________________

discover ______________________

confirm ______________________

alligator ______________________

purple ______________________

Arkansas ______________________

fern ______________________

thirsty ______________________

northern ______________________

return ______________________

cougar ______________________

western ______________________

Virginia ______________________

forest ______________________

urban ______________________

NAME ______________________________

Lesson 10 r-Controlled Vowels: ar, er, ir, or, ur

Words in Context

Write spelling words to complete the following paragraph. You will not use all of the words.

Challenge

Circle other **r**-controlled vowels you find in the paragraph.

Cougars

A __________________ is another name for a mountain lion. Cougars used to live all over the continental U.S., including __________________ and __________________. Now, they are now found mostly in the __________________ deserts of the U.S. They have been forced out of their natural habitats because of __________________ growth.

Cougars are born with spots, but the spots soon fade to a gray, yellow, or brown color. Once cougars __________________ prey, they sneak up quietly and pounce. Since cougars are generally solitary animals, if there is more than one set of tracks, you can __________________ that it is usually a mother and her cubs. If they get separated, the cubs often __________________ to where they ate last to find their mother.

Word Building

Prefixes are groups of letters added to the beginning of words to change the meaning of the words. A common prefix is **re-**. The prefix **re-** means *again* or *back*.

The spelling word *return* means *to go back* or *to take back*. Write the two other words from the spelling list you can add **re** to.

__________________ __________________

NAME ____________________

Lesson 10 r-Controlled Vowels: **ar, er, ir, or, ur**

Fun with Words

In Column A, fill in the blanks with a spelling word. In Column B, fill in your own answers.

Column A

1. Jim's favorite color is ____________________.
2. Meranda lives in an ____________________.
3. Johnny would like to ____________________ a hidden treasure.
4. Charlotte was born in the state of ____________________.
5. Lisa now lives in the state of ____________________.
6. When Mike exercises, he becomes ____________________.
7. Yoshki's favorite reptile is an ____________________.
8. Sylvia's favorite plant is the ____________________.
9. The nurse will ____________________ the appointment.
10. Phoebe lives in the city, an ____________________ setting.

Column B

1. My favorite color is ____________________.
2. I live in a/an ____________________.
3. I would like to ____________________ a ____________________.
4. I was born in the state of ____________________.
5. I now live in the state of ____________________.
6. When I exercise I become ____________________.
7. My favorite reptile is a/an ____________________.
8. My favorite plant is the ____________________.
9. I will ____________________ the test date with my teacher.
10. I live in the ____________________.

NAME ____________________

Lesson 10 r-Controlled Vowels: ar, er, ir, or, ur

Words in Writing

Write a paragraph about a career you may want to pursue. Use at least four words from the box in your paragraph.

apartment	**alligator**	**fern**	**return**	**Virginia**
discover	**purple**	**thirsty**	**cougar**	**forest**
confirm	**Arkansas**	**northern**	**western**	**urban**

____

____

____

____

____

____

Using the Dictionary

Guide words are the first and last word on a dictionary page. They appear at the top of each page. All words on that page fall between those two words. Look up the guide words for the following words and write them below.

1. alligator ____________ ____________
2. apartment ____________ ____________
3. confirm ____________ ____________
4. cougar ____________ ____________
5. fern ____________ ____________
6. forest ____________ ____________
7. purple ____________ ____________
8. urban ____________ ____________

NAME ______________________________

Lesson 11 Special Spelling Patterns: **ough, augh**

Say each word out loud. Then, write the words on the lines provided.

Spelling Tip	Spelling patterns **ough** and **augh** have the same short **o** sound (found in *dog*), as the /al/, /au/, and /aw/ sounds.

Spelling Words

aught ______________________

bought ______________________

caught ______________________

brought ______________________

daughter ______________________

cough ______________________

distraught ______________________

fought ______________________

fraught ______________________

ought ______________________

naught ______________________

sought ______________________

taught ______________________

thought ______________________

trough ______________________

NAME ________________________

Lesson 11 Special Spelling Patterns: **ough, augh**

Words in Context

Complete the following poem with spelling words.

Chloe's Cough

Chloe ________________ a cold.

She couldn't stop her ________________.

Chloe ________________ a cure.

She became so ________________.

Chloe ________________ to rest and sleep,

So her mother ________________.

She ________________ her ________________ oranges

And special teas she ________________.

Finally, Chloe ________________ her cold

When she did just what her mother ________________.

Word Building

Homophones are words that sound alike but have different spellings and meanings. Find the two spelling words that are homophones. Write the words and use a dictionary to write their definitions.

________________ ____

____

________________ ____

____

NAME ________________________

Lesson 11 Special Spelling Patterns: **ough, augh**

Fun with Words

Complete the puzzle using spelling words.

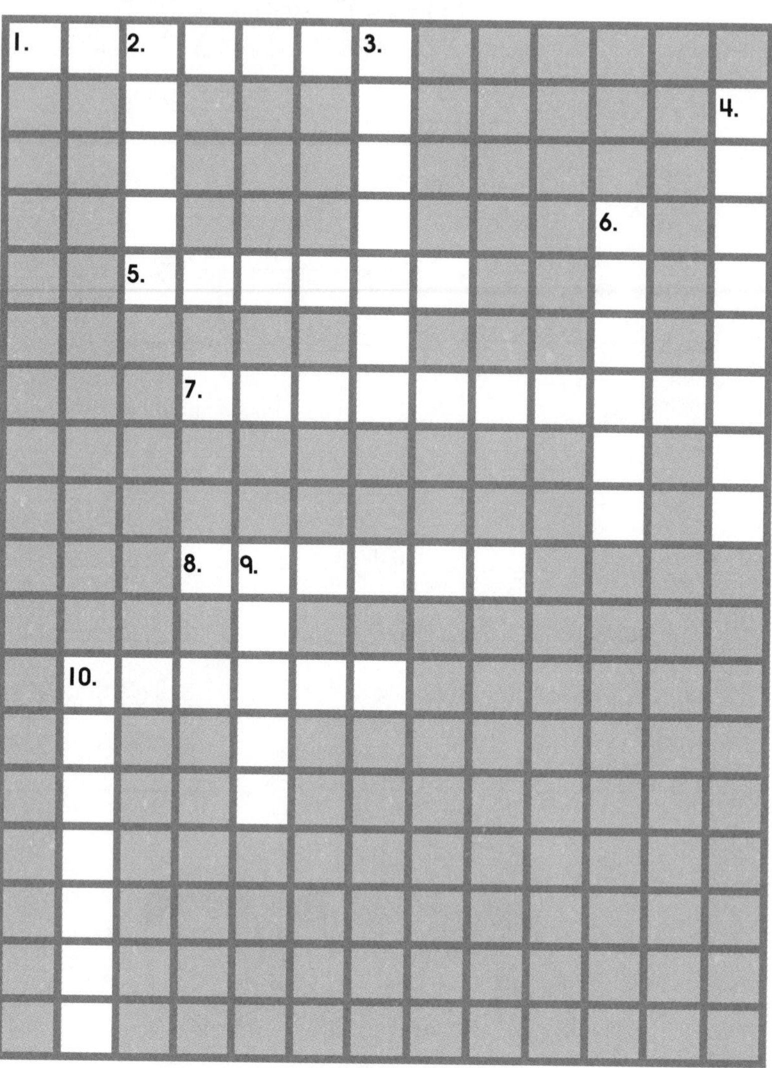

Across

1. An adjective meaning *filled* or *loaded.*
5. A noun meaning *a long, narrow open container.*
7. An adjective meaning *very confused* or *troubled by worry.*
8. A verb that is the past tense of *seek.*
10. A verb that is the past tense of *buy.*

Down

2. A pronoun meaning *anything at all.*
3. A verb that is the past tense of *think.*
4. A noun meaning *a girl or woman as she relates to a parent.*
6. A noun meaning *the same as nothing.*
9. A helping verb meaning *to be forced by what is right or necessary.*
10. A verb that is the past tense of *bring.*

NAME ______________________

Lesson 11 Special Spelling Patterns: **ough, augh**

Words in Writing

Write a poem using as many spelling words as you can. The poem can be funny or serious.

____

____

____

____

____

____

____

____

____

____

____

Misspelled Words

Circle the misspelled words and write them correctly on the lines.

What Is a Cold?

A cold is an infection of the nose and throat. A cold comes from a variety of viruses. A virus is a matter that multiplies and lives in cells causing diseases. Colds oght to last about a week, but they sometimes last longer. People who work closely with others who have colds often become distraut because colds are very contagious. Colds are cought through inhaling and touching others who are infected. A caugh, a runny nose, and a scratchy throat are all thaught to be symptoms of a cold. One who has a cold owght to get plenty of rest and fluids.

______________ ______________ ______________

______________ ______________ ______________

NAME ______________________________

Review Lessons 9–11

Write each of the following words on the lines provided. Circle the vowel dipthongs /ou/ and /oy/. Then, underline the final /əl/ vowel combination.

1. foundation ____________________
2. annoy ____________________
3. cancel ____________________
4. our ____________________
5. loyal ____________________
6. label ____________________

LESSONS 9–11 REVIEW

Write each of the following spelling words on the lines. Circle the letters that make the short **o** sound found in *dog*.

1. chalk ____________________
2. author ____________________
3. crawl ____________________
4. caught ____________________
5. fought ____________________
6. false ____________________
7. autograph ____________________
8. lawn ____________________
9. taught ____________________
10. thought ____________________

Complete the following sentences with words from the above list.

1. The students drew their hopscotch marks with ____________________.
2. The famous ____________________ signed an ____________________.
3. After the rain, we had a bright green ____________________.
4. The umpire wasn't sure where the ball was ____________________.
5. The best friends were sorry that they ____________________.

NAME ____________________

Review Lessons 9–11

Write each of the following spelling words on the lines. Circle the **r**-controlled vowels (including the **r**).

1. cougar ____________	**6.** apartment ____________
2. western ____________	**7.** confirm ____________
3. Virginia ____________	**8.** purple ____________
4. forest ____________	**9.** fern ____________
5. urban ____________	**10.** northern ____________

Complete the following paragraph with words from above.

The beautiful state of ____________ is located in the eastern part of the United States. Eastern Virginia, on the coast of the Atlantic Ocean, has many ____________ areas. Some Eastern Virginia cities are close to Washington, D.C. ____________ Virginia is mountainous. The Allegheny and Blue Ridge Mountains run through this part of Virginia. A beautiful Virginia ____________ is the perfect place for hiking, picnicking, and observing nature. Virginia is beautiful during all four of its amazing seasons.

NAME ______________________

Lesson 12 Compound Words

Say each of the following words out loud. Then, write each word.

Spelling Tip	**Compound words** are made by joining two words. Compound words may or may not join the meanings of the two words.

Spelling Words

applesauce ____________

baseball ____________

blueprint ____________

bookshelf ____________

cupcake ____________

daylight ____________

drawbridge ____________

grandparents ____________

haircut ____________

horseback ____________

housework ____________

mailbox ____________

sunset ____________

textbook ____________

volleyball ____________

NAME ____________________

Lesson 12 Compound Words

Challenge

Circle any other compound words you find.

Words in Context

Complete the following sentences with spelling words.

1. Peter likes a __________ made with __________ instead of sugar.
2. Elise's favorite activity is __________ riding on her uncle's farm.
3. When my parents finish the __________ and I finish my homework, we're going to the movies.
4. On my birthday, the __________ was stuffed with cards.
5. During __________ savings time, the __________ comes later in the day.
6. The architect is putting the finishing touches on the building's __________.
7. Dennis loves sports and plays both __________ and 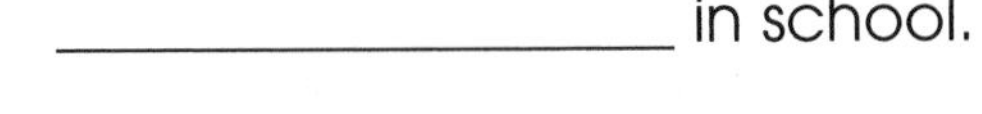 in school.

8. My __________ told me about their visit to Port Clinton, where they saw a __________ and tall sailboats.
9. The teacher asked Billy to put his __________ back on the __________.
10. Andy's dad gets a __________ at the barbershop in town.

NAME ____________________

Lesson 12 Compound Words

Fun with Words

Make new compounds words by adding a word to each word below. Use a dictionary if you need help.

1. blue + ______________ = ______________
2. book + ______________ = ______________
3. cup + ______________ = ______________
4. ______________ + light = ______________
5. grand + ______________ = ______________

Words Across the Curriculum

Write each science word on the lines below.

1. aftershock ______________
2. earthquake ______________
3. inside ______________
4. outside ______________
5. underground ______________

Complete the following paragraph with science words from above.

Earthquakes

An ______________ is a shaking of the ground. Earthquakes are caused by the shifting of ______________ rock or from the action of a volcano. Shifting and moving rocks cause vibrations. An ______________ can be felt toward the end of the movement of earthquakes. If you live close to an area where earthquakes are likely to occur, it is a good idea to have a safety plan. If you are ______________, stay outside. If you are ______________, try to get to a doorway, under a sturdy table, or by an interior wall. Knowing what to do during an earthquake is very important.

NAME ______________________

Lesson 12 Compound Words

Words in Writing
Using at least five spelling words, write a paragraph describing your family.

____
____
____
____
____
____
____
____
____
____
____
____

Using a Dictionary
Use a dictionary to look up the definitions of the following individual words and compound words. Then, use each word in a sentence.

1. blue ______________________
2. print ______________________
3. blueprint ______________________
4. draw ______________________
5. bridge ______________________
6. drawbridge ______________________

NAME ______________________________

Lesson 13 Contractions

Say each of the following contractions out loud. Then, write each word.

Spelling Tip	**Contractions** are shortened forms of words. The words are shortened by leaving out letters and replacing them with an apostrophe.

Spelling Words

I'll ____________________

I'm ____________________

she's ____________________

that's ____________________

they're ____________________

what's ____________________

you're ____________________

he'd ____________________

I've ____________________

we've ____________________

can't ____________________

don't ____________________

weren't ____________________

wouldn't ____________________

let's ____________________

NAME ______________________

Lesson 13 Contractions

Words in Context

The following dialogue contains words that could be written as contractions. Change the words to contractions from the spelling word list. Write them above the existing words.

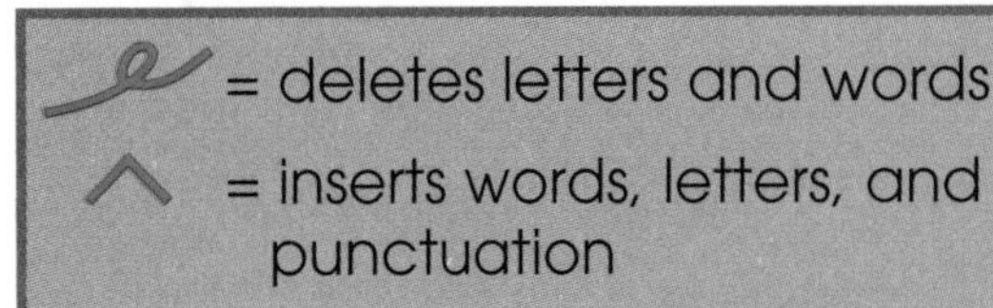

= deletes letters and words
= inserts words, letters, and punctuation

"Hey, Leigh, where are you running off to so fast?" asked Melissa.

"I am late for a meeting," answered Leigh.

"You are late for a meeting? What kind of meeting?" asked Melissa.

"I will talk as we walk," Leigh said smiling. "I do not have much time. I am going to a Sierra Club meeting."

"What is that?" asked Melissa.

"You do not know what the Sierra Club is?" asked Leigh. "The Sierra Club is America's oldest and largest environmental organization. We have been studying American explorers in school. Do you remember John Muir?" He was from Scotland, but he came to America and walked all over the country. He would stop along the way and take notes about all the wonderful things he saw in nature. He wanted to make sure that our natural environment was around for many generations."

Melissa responded, "That is right, I remember. He's considered the founder of our National Park System."

"You are right," said Leigh. "He is also the founder of the Sierra Club. The members work for clean water, safe forests, and clean air, among other issues. You would not believe some of the activities I have joined. I feel really good doing it."

"Well, let us get moving," chimed in Melissa. "We can not be late!"

NAME ______________________

Lesson 13 Contractions

Fun with Words

Connect the words to make contractions. Draw a line from each of the words in Line 1 to any of the words in Line 2 that might follow them. (For example, in the first Line 1, *he* would not go with *am*, but *he* would go with *is*.) Then, write the contractions that these words make on Line 3. Make as may contractions as you can.

Line 1: I he she you we they it that could should would

Line 2: am is tonight are was space were

Line 3: ______________________

____

Line 1: I he she you we they it that could should would

Line 2: had have shoe

Line 3: ______________________

____

Line 1: can do were would

Line 2: giraffe not should Oliver

Line 3: ______________________

____

NAME ____________________

Lesson 13 Contractions

Words in Writing

Write a dialogue between at least two characters about a school activity or community activity. Use at least six of the contractions from this lesson.

____

____

____

____

____

____

____

Misspelled Words

Some of the contractions in the following sentences are either misspelled or the apostrophe is in the wrong place. Circle the incorrect contractions and write them correctly on the lines provided.

1. Ashley and Megan cann't believe they're advancing to the finals of the spelling bee. ____________
2. Will said h'ed pick up dinner on the way home from track practice. ____________
3. Tasha said, "I'hve been waiting for weeks for this movie to open." ____________
4. Leah said she'is excited about the upcoming softball season. ____________
5. Mr. Pickney's students said they'r joining a community clean-up program for their special project this semester. ____________
6. Nicole and Chris wer'ent quite ready for school when the bus pulled up. ____________
7. Whats' the name of your favorite song? ____________
8. The banker would'nt accept the out of town check. ____________

NAME ______________________

Review Lessons 12–13

Write each of the following spelling words. Circle the two individual words that make up the compound words. Circle the apostrophes in the contractions.

1. applesauce ______________
2. I'm ______________
3. blueprint ______________
4. that's ______________
5. cupcake ______________
6. what's ______________
7. drawbridge ______________
8. he'd ______________
9. haircut ______________
10. we've ______________
11. housework ______________
12. don't ______________
13. sunset ______________
14. wouldn't ______________
15. volleyball ______________
16. I'll ______________
17. textbook ______________
18. let's ______________
19. baseball ______________
20. she's ______________

LESSONS 12–13 REVIEW

NAME ____________________

Review Lessons 12–13

Below is a blueprint for a house where some Olympic athletes will live. Most of the places are labeled, but four outside areas are not. Choose words from Word Box A to label the unlabeled outside areas.

Word Box A	
	baseball bookshelf daylight drawbridge grandparents housework mailbox sunset volleyball

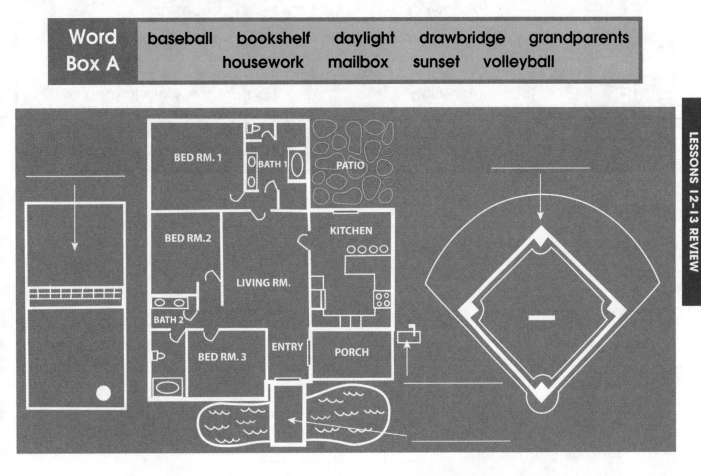

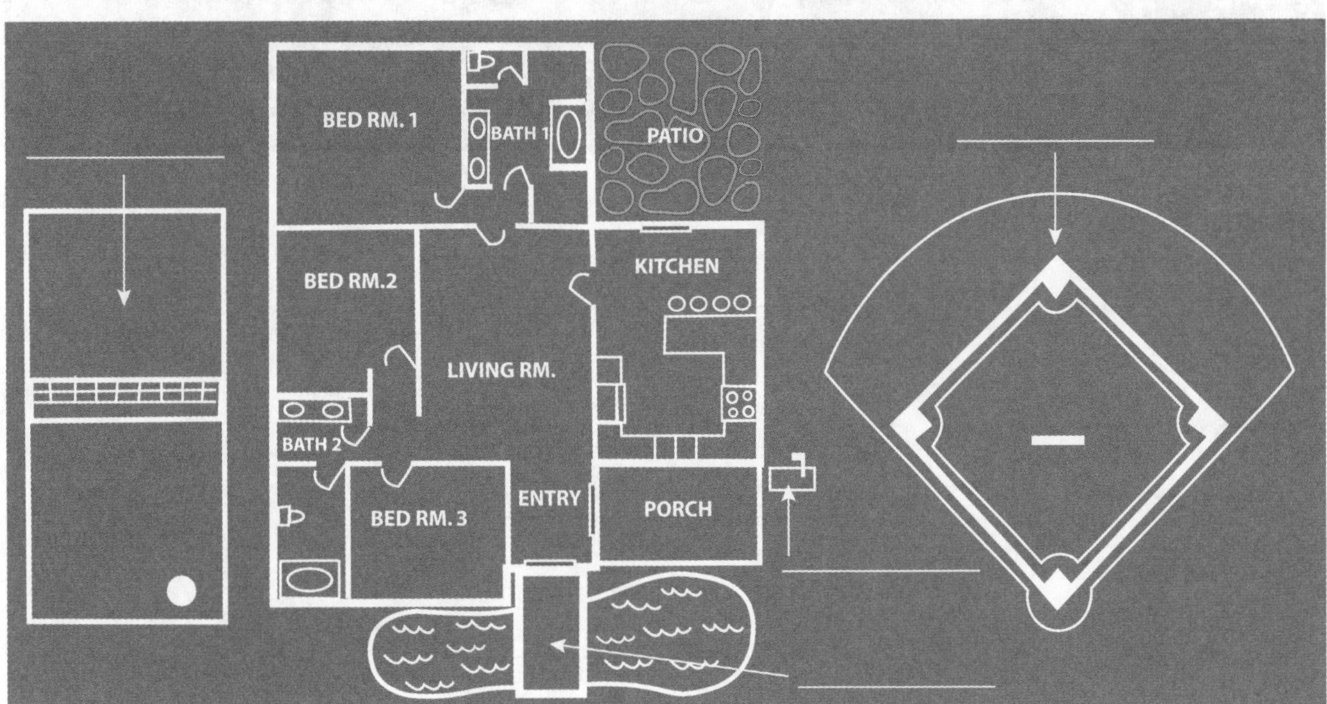

LESSONS 12-13 REVIEW

Use each of the remaining words in Word Box A in a sentence as it might relate to the above house. Add contractions from Word Box B to at least three of your sentences. One has been done for you.

Word Box B	
	can't let's that's wouldn't you're

1. We can't see the sunset from the kitchen.
2. ____________________
3. ____________________
4. ____________________
5. ____________________

NAME ____________________

Lesson 14 Regular Plural Nouns

Say each of the following plural nouns out loud. Then, write each word.

Spelling Tip

Following are the rules for making nouns plural:

Most nouns are made plural by adding **s** to the singular form.
Nouns ending in **s**, **x**, **z**, **ch**, and **sh** are made by adding **es**.
Nouns ending in **y** with a vowel before the **y** are formed by adding an **s**.
Nouns ending in **y** with a consonant before the **y** are formed by changing the **y** to **i** and adding **es**.
Nouns ending in **o** with a vowel before the **o** are formed by adding **s**.
Nouns ending in **o** with a consonant before the **o** are formed by adding **es**.

Spelling Words

friends ____________________

passes ____________________

taxes ____________________

buzzes ____________________

benches ____________________

bushes ____________________

donkeys ____________________

batteries ____________________

patios ____________________

echoes ____________________

pictures ____________________

valleys ____________________

centuries ____________________

radios ____________________

tomatoes ____________________

NAME ____________________

Lesson 14 Regular Plural Nouns

Words in Context

Complete the following narrative with spelling words. Not all of the words will be used.

Challenge

Find other regular plural words in the narrative and circle them.

Mary, Jim, Robyn, Peter, Christina, and Robert were best ________________. They had known each other since first grade. On the last day of fifth grade, they sat on some ________________, talking about the last year.

"Remember the time Robert crashed his model airplane into the ________________, and we all searched and searched for hours?" asked Robyn. "It seemed like it took ________________ to find, but we ended up having a blast."

"How about the time we all tried making spaghetti in Mary's mom's kitchen?" said Jim. "We had crushed ________________ all over everything!"

"I'm really going to miss Mrs. Bell in science class. She didn't even mind when we set up all of those ________________ to try to break the sound barrier," said Peter.

"She even brought us more ________________," added Jim.

"I'll especially miss Mrs. Richardson's field trips," commented Mary. "I'll never forget our hiking trip. We even got to ride ________________. The mountains and the ________________ were so beautiful".

"Do you remember how she had all of us try to yodel so we could hear our ________________?" laughed Robert.

"Well, we better go," sighed Christina. "It's almost time for class ________________."

"Then," continued Jim, "we're off to climb our next mountain."

NAME ____________________

Lesson 14 Regular Plural Nouns

Fun with Words
Find all of the spelling words from the lesson in the puzzle below. The words can be horizontal, vertical, diagonal, forward, and backward.

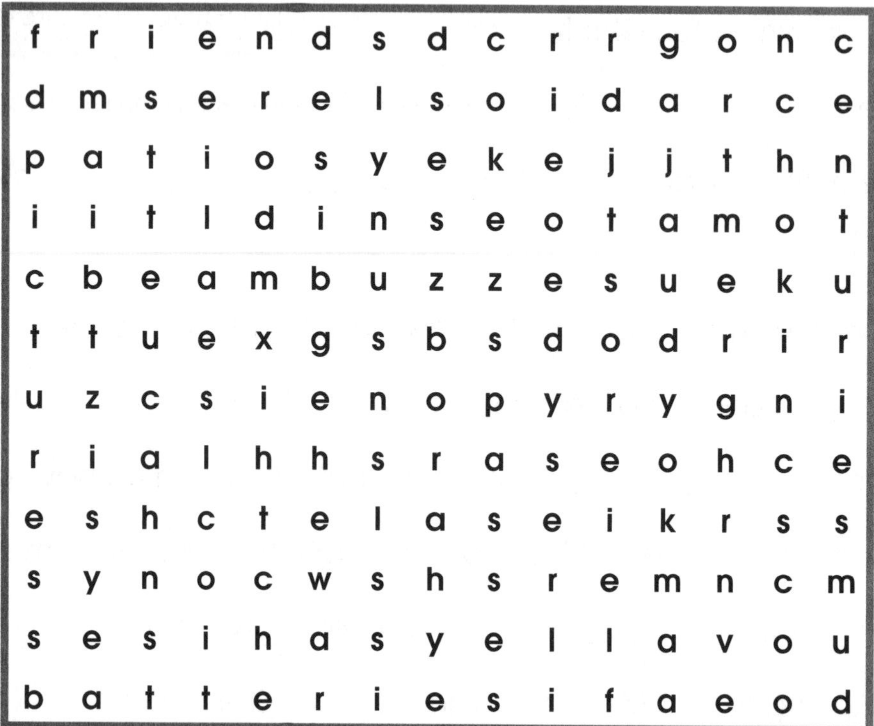

f	r	i	e	n	d	s	d	c	r	r	g	o	n	c
d	m	s	e	r	e	l	s	o	i	d	a	r	c	e
p	a	t	i	o	s	y	e	k	e	j	j	t	h	n
i	i	t	l	d	i	n	s	e	o	t	a	m	o	t
c	b	e	a	m	b	u	z	z	e	s	u	e	k	u
t	t	u	e	x	g	s	b	s	d	o	d	r	i	r
u	z	c	s	i	e	n	o	p	y	r	y	g	n	i
r	i	a	l	h	h	s	r	a	s	e	o	h	c	e
e	s	h	c	t	e	l	a	s	e	i	k	r	s	s
s	y	n	o	c	w	s	h	s	r	e	m	n	c	m
s	e	s	i	h	a	s	y	e	l	l	a	v	o	u
b	a	t	t	e	r	i	e	s	i	f	a	e	o	d

Words Across the Curriculum 
Write each social studies word on the lines below.

1. animals ____________________
2. doctors ____________________
3. heroes ____________________
4. officers ____________________
5. teachers ____________________

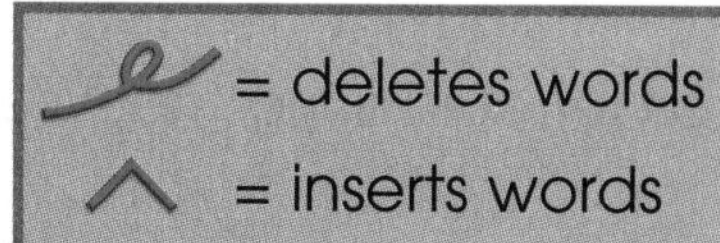

Correct the words in the paragraph below by writing the correct spelling above them.

Some people have professions that may make them heros. Firefighters, police officeres, doctores, and veterinarians can all be heros. Teacheres can be heroes by teaching us to do our best, and inspire us to be even better. Animales can be heros, too. Dogs have saved their guardians from burning houses and have brought sick guardians medication.

NAME ___________________________

Lesson 14 Regular Plural Nouns

Words in Writing

Write a paragraph describing who has been a hero in your life. Use at least five words from this lesson.

____

____

____

____

____

____

____

____

Using a Dictionary

Write the following words from this lesson in alphabetical order.

friends	bushes
pictures	animals
passes	donkeys
valleys	doctors
taxes	batteries
centuries	heroes
buzzes	patios
radios	officers
benches	echoes
tomatoes	teachers

1. ____________ 11. ____________
2. ____________ 12. ____________
3. ____________ 13. ____________
4. ____________ 14. ____________
5. ____________ 15. ____________
6. ____________ 16. ____________
7. ____________ 17. ____________
8. ____________ 18. ____________
9. ____________ 19. ____________
10. ____________ 20. ____________

NAME ______________________

Lesson 15 Irregular Plural Nouns

Say each of the following plural nouns out loud. Then, write each word.

Spelling Tip

Some nouns do not have a regular pattern to form their plurals. These plural nouns must be memorized.

Spelling Words

children ______________________

deer ______________________

dozen ______________________

feet ______________________

geese ______________________

media ______________________

men ______________________

mice ______________________

moose ______________________

oxen ______________________

sheep ______________________

teeth ______________________

traffic ______________________

wheat ______________________

women ______________________

NAME __________________________

Lesson 15 Irregular Plural Nouns

Words in Context

Complete the following sentences using spelling words.

1. Since one child got to go, all of the ____________ wanted to go, too.
2. I saw one deer in the woods, and then I saw three more ____________ pass by.
3. Hally got one dozen roses for Valentine's Day, and Drea received two ____________.
4. Matt jumped one foot in the contest, and then he tried again and he jumped four ____________.

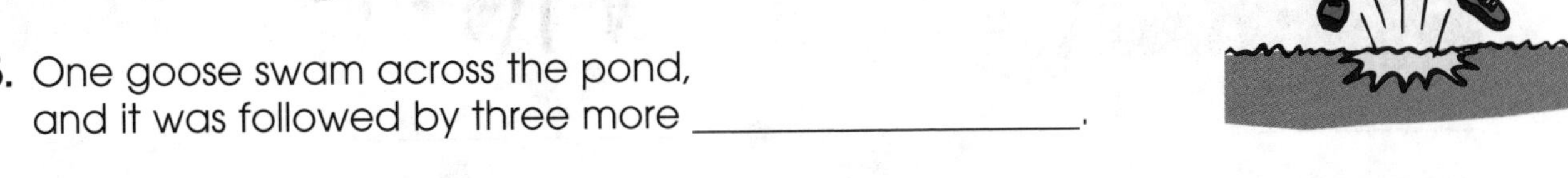

5. One goose swam across the pond, and it was followed by three more ____________.
6. Television is one of the most popular mediums of all ____________.
7. One man wasn't enough to hold up the beam—it took three ____________.
8. One mouse snatched the cheese, and then two more ____________ got the crumbs.
9. Alexandra saw not one moose but two ____________ in the woods.
10. One ox was not enough to pull the cart; it took two ____________.
11. Cindy saw a sheep on the hill, and then she saw a dozen ____________ in the field.
12. Tommy's tooth hurt, so his parents had his ____________ examined by the dentist.
13. The traffic today was heavy, but the ____________ is heavy every day.
14. One grain of wheat is not enough to make a bowl of cereal, it will take many grains of ____________.
15. One woman jumped in the airport taxi, and then three more ____________ jumped in, too.

NAME ______________________

Lesson 15 Irregular Plural Nouns

Fun with Words

Under each picture, write the spelling word that matches.

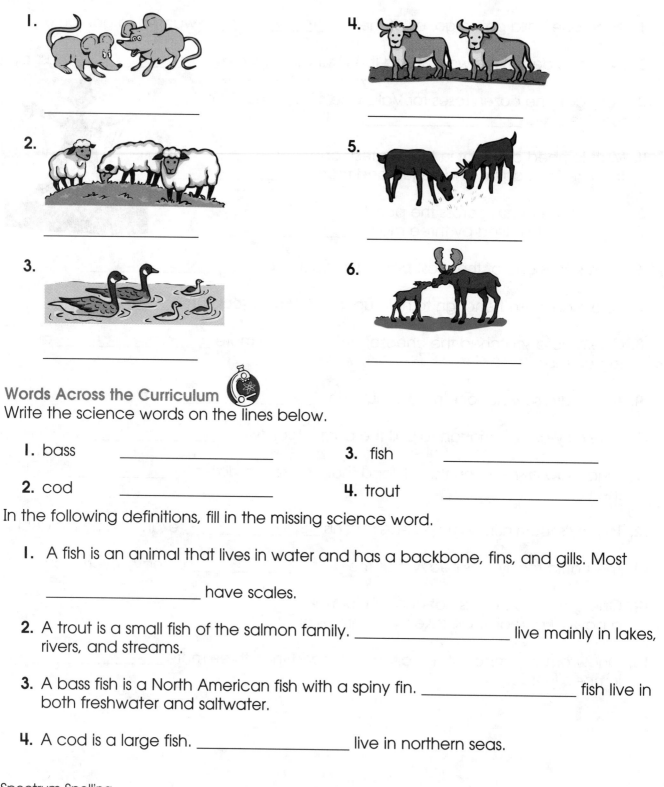

1. 

____

2. 

____

3. 

____

4. 

____

5. 

____

6. 

____

Words Across the Curriculum

Write the science words on the lines below.

1. bass ______________________
2. cod ______________________
3. fish ______________________
4. trout ______________________

In the following definitions, fill in the missing science word.

1. A fish is an animal that lives in water and has a backbone, fins, and gills. Most ______________________ have scales.
2. A trout is a small fish of the salmon family. ______________________ live mainly in lakes, rivers, and streams.
3. A bass fish is a North American fish with a spiny fin. ______________________ fish live in both freshwater and saltwater.
4. A cod is a large fish. ______________________ live in northern seas.

NAME ____________________

Lesson 15 Irregular Plural Nouns

Words in Writing

Write six sentences using at least one word from this lesson in each.

1. ____________________
2. ____________________
3. ____________________
4. ____________________
5. ____________________
6. ____________________

Misspelled Words

The following narrative contains nine misspelled words from this lesson. Cross out the misspelled words and write the correct spellings above them.

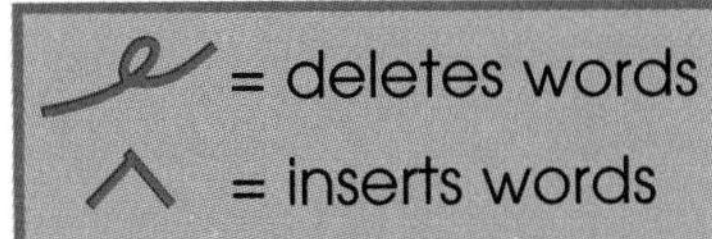

The childrens in Mrs. McGuire's 5th grade class were excited to visit the Wildlife Rehabilitation Center. A wildlife rehabilitation center is a place that takes in injured wild animals and treats and cares for them until they are ready to be released back to their habitats. While at the center, the children were able to see deers, gooses, sheeps, and even tiny mices. The director of the center told the childrens that all of the animals will be treated and cared for until they are better. The children learned that donations are accepted to help the center buy equipment and pay those who work at the center. Sometimes, they have fundraisers and the mediums attends and spreads the word to the community to help raise money. The children also learned another way to help the center. Mans, womans, and even children can volunteer at the center. The children left feeling happy that there are places to care for these injured animals and also glad to know that they will be able to help, too.

NAME ____________________

Lesson 16 Possessives

Say each of the following possessive nouns out loud. Then, write each word.

Spelling Tip

Possessives show ownership.
To spell the possessive of a singular noun, add an apostrophe and **s**.
My aunt**'s** cookies are the best.

To spell the possessive of plural nouns ending in **s**, simply add the apostrophe.
All of the brother**s'** T-shirts were in the laundry room.

If the plural noun does not end in an **s**, add both the apostrophe and **s**.
All of the deer**'s** antlers were starting to grow.

Spelling Words

bicyclist's ____________________

bicyclists' ____________________

child's ____________________

children's ____________________

grandfather's ____________________

grandfathers' ____________________

grandmother's ____________________

grandmothers' ____________________

principal's ____________________

principals' ____________________

sister's ____________________

sisters' ____________________

uncle's ____________________

uncles' ____________________

today's ____________________

NAME ____________________

Lesson 16 Possessives

Words in Context

Add an apostrophe in the correct place to each word in parentheses to make it possessive. Then, write it on the line.

Thursday, March 24

I am so excited! Spring break is just around the corner, and I'm going to my aunt and (uncle) ________________ house for the whole week. I can't wait to see Buffy, their dog. She's my pal. She is a beagle, and she loves to play. She even likes to take (childrens) ________________ toys and build little forts out of them.

My grandfather and grandmother will come to visit when I'm there. My (grandmothers) ________________ blackberry bread is delicious, and she promised she would bring some for me. My uncle loves to play baseball, and he said he would play catch with me. I have four uncles, and all of my (uncles) ________________ old sports equipment will be there.

My grandfather promised me a surprise. But I think I know what it is. My parents got me a bicycle for my birthday last week. I think my grandparents will get me a (bicyclists) ________________ helmet and gloves. Then, I'll be ready to ride! (Todays) ________________ paper says the weather is going to be perfect. I can't wait for spring break!

NAME ______________________

Lesson 16 Possessives

Fun with Words

Choose a spelling word that belongs in each sentence and fits in the boxes. Write the words in the boxes. Apostrophes get their own box.

1. My ________________ office is on the first floor of the school.

2. The ________________ coloring book was in his backpack.

3. Last night's sports scores are in ________________ newspaper.

4. All of the ________________ helmets were the same style.

5. Emma liked to borrow her oldest ________________ clothes.

6. All of my aunt and ________________ houses are in Arizona.

7. My grandfather and ________________ recipes are from their ancestors.

8. The ________________ jersey got muddy from the puddles.

9. The ________________ toys were in the play box.

10. All of the bride's brothers' vests and ________________ dresses were ready.

NAME ______________________

Lesson 16 Possessives

Words in Writing

Write a journal entry about something you have done recently. Use at least five possessive words in your entry.

____

____

____

____

____

____

Using a Dictionary

Write the definition of each spelling word below. Then, use each word in a sentence.

1. bicyclist's ______________________

____

2. bicyclists' ______________________

____

3. child's ______________________

____

4. children's ______________________

____

5. grandfather's ______________________

____

6. grandfathers' ______________________

____

NAME ____________________

Review Lessons 14–16

Write each of the following words on the lines provided. For the regular plurals, circle the **s** or **es** that makes the word plural. Do not circle anything in the irregular plurals.

1. benches ____________
2. bushes ____________
3. centuries ____________
4. deer ____________
5. echoes ____________
6. fish ____________
7. friends ____________
8. geese ____________
9. moose ____________
10. oxen ____________
11. passes ____________
12. radios ____________
13. sheep ____________
14. taxes ____________
15. valleys ____________

LESSONS 14–16 REVIEW

Some of the words from the above list are misspelled in the following paragraph. Cross out the misspelled words and rewrite them correctly above the misspelled word.

Denali National Park

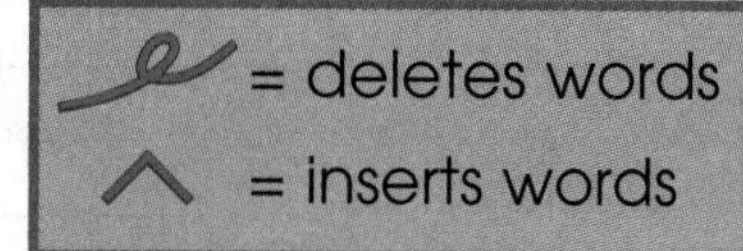

Mt. McKinley's highest peak is 20,320 feet, the highest point in America. This mountain is located in Denali National Park in Alaska. Many amazing wonders reside in this national park. Monumental glaciers dot the area. Its slopes and valleyes are covered with lakes, rivers, and streams that remain from the glaciers that retreated centurys ago. More than 650 species of plants live in Denali. Wildlife is abundant. More than 39 species of mammals, 167 species of birds, and 10 species of fishs dwell in this wonderland. Some of the most common mammals found are mooses, sheeps, bears, wolves, oxes, deers, and elk. Visitors can take part in many activities, including wildlife viewing, hiking, mountaineering, backcountry camping, skiing, and attending naturalistic lectures and programs.

NAME ____________________

Review Lessons 14–16

Write each of the following words on the lines provided. Circle the apostrophe or the apostrophe and **s** that make the words possessive.

1. bicyclists' ____________________

2. child's ____________________

3. children's ____________________

4. grandfathers' ____________________

5. principal's ____________________

6. sisters' ____________________

7. uncle's ____________________

8. today's ____________________

The words in the above list are scrambled in the following sentences. Unscramble and write them on the lines following each sentence.

1. The teacher asked her students to write ytoda's date on their papers. ____________________

2. All of the sr'siste pictures were in the yearbook. ____________________

3. The csh'inledr books were on the lower shelf. ____________________

4. My clneu's classic car is a beautiful matte yellow. ____________________

5. The main nplr'scpiai goal was the education and well being of her students. ____________________

6. My rnftes'gadahr umbrella was in the hall closet, next to his coat. ____________________

7. The clybi'tsisc bags were filled with water, bananas, bagels, and power bars for her bike ride later that day. ____________________

8. Brook's daughter ordered the lc'hids meal. ____________________

LESSONS 14–16 REVIEW

NAME ______________________

Lesson 17 Prefixes: dis-, pre-, un-

Say each of the following words out loud. Then, write each word.

Spelling Tip

A **prefix** is a group of letters that is added to the beginning of a base word to change its meaning. The prefix **dis**– means *opposite*. The prefix **pre**– means *before*. The prefix **un**– means *not*.

Spelling Words

disappoint ______________________

prepaid ______________________

unable ______________________

disapprove ______________________

prerecorded ______________________

unbeaten ______________________

discover ______________________

preset ______________________

unhappy ______________________

dishonest ______________________

preschool ______________________

unlimited ______________________

disorder ______________________

pretest ______________________

unsure ______________________

NAME ______________________

Lesson 17 Prefixes: **dis-**, **pre-**, **un-**

Words in Context

Complete the following narrative by filling in the blanks with spelling words. You may use some words more than once.

The room was in ________________. Alicia didn't want to ________________ her parents. But how was she going to clean up this mess before her parents got home from picking up her brother at ________________? At first, Alicia's parents had said, "We ________________ of you having a puppy right now." They thought she would be ________________ to take care of a puppy and keep up with her studies. She understood how important it was to care for a pet. Her parents showed an ________________ amount of patience and understanding, and she was eventually allowed to get one.

Alicia was running late for volleyball practice when she left that morning. Now, she had to find her textbook to study for a ________________. "If my parents ________________ I've let things go, they'll never trust me again," Alicia said to her new puppy, Buzz. Buzz scampered over to her desk, pulled off an envelope, and brought it to Alicia. "I forgot, I got this from the animal shelter. It's a flyer for puppy training classes and a ________________ envelope. I was ________________ about taking you to training, but you may be right," she said.

Alicia heard her parents pull up in the driveway. "Well, they may be ________________ about my room, but I think they will be happy with our decision!"

NAME ______________________

Lesson 17 Prefixes: **dis-**, **pre-**, **un-**

Fun with Words

Solve the following rhymes with a spelling word.

1. Tana was so happy; she just passed the test.
Alex was not happy; he did not do his best.

Alex was ________________.

2. Donald had to pay the bill as it was overdue.
Richard's bill was paid before by his friend Drew.

Richard's bill was ________________.

3. Courtney was able to stay on top and make the gymnastics team.
Vanessa did well on the bars but was not able to stay on the beam.

Vanessa was ________________ to stay on the beam.

Words Across the Curriculum

Write the history words on the lines.

1. disagree ________________

2. dispute ________________

3. preamble ________________

Choose words from the list above to complete the following paragraph.

The U.S. Constitution is a document in which the laws and rules of the United States are recorded. The U.S. Constitution was drawn up and signed in 1787. The constitution consists of seven articles, a ________________ that comes before the constitution and explains its purpose, and 27 amendments have been added afterward. Some people have found the wording of the U.S. Constitution to be unclear and open to interpretation. A ________________ existed over the power between the union and states rights. To this day, some people ________________ about the meaning of the U.S. Constitution.

NAME ____________________

Lesson 17 Prefixes: dis-, pre-, un-

Words in Writing

Write a short, descriptive narrative with at least two characters. Use at least five words from this lesson in your narrative. You can also use other words with the prefixes **dis**–, **pre**–, or **un**–.

____

____

____

____

____

____

____

____

____

____

Misspelled Words

The prefixes in Column A are all mixed up. Rewrite the words in Column B with the correct prefixes.

Column A	Column B
1. unhonest	____________
2. disrecorded	____________
3. disbeaten	____________
4. precover	____________
5. disset	____________
6. dislimited	____________

NAME ______________________

Lesson 18 Suffixes: -ion, -tion, -ation

Say each of the following words out loud. Then, write each word.

Spelling Tip

A **suffix** is a group of letters that are added to the end of a base word to change its meaning. The suffixes -**ion**, -**tion**, and -**ation** mean *the state or quality of.*

Spelling Words

ambition ______________________

instruction ______________________

admiration ______________________

champion ______________________

interception ______________________

appreciation ______________________

companion ______________________

production ______________________

education ______________________

conclusion ______________________

rejection ______________________

imagination ______________________

possession ______________________

tradition ______________________

preparation ______________________

NAME ____________________

Lesson 18 Suffixes: -ion, -tion, -ation

Words in Context

Some of the spelling words are scrambled in the following biography. Unscramble the words and rewrite them above the scrambled words.

Mikhail Baryshnikov

It takes talent and a lot of practice. It takes bmntiaoi and gamtaininio. It also takes some luck. Becoming a famous dancer is not easy. One of the world's most famous dancers is Mikhail Baryshnikov. Born in Russia in 1948, Baryshnikov danced with the Kirov Ballet in Russia until 1974. He was highly respected and held the tmraidoani of the Russian people. He defected to America in 1974 and joined the American Ballet Theatre and the New York City Ballet. He has performed and choreographed many ballets. He won the prcainapeito of the American audiences through his work in theatre, movies, and television. Baryshnikov also tours with his own modern dance poutonicdr company. The Baryshnikov Dance Foundation supports new and mid-career dancers, musicians, and other artists in training and developing their crafts. Baryshnikov's intense niaaepotrrp for his art and his powerful and graceful performances have brought him a life long career and devoted audiences.

NAME ______________________

Lesson 18 Suffixes: -ion, -tion, -ation

Fun with Words

Choose a spelling word that completes each sentence.

1. The football team was the ______________ of the state.
2. It is a popular ______________ to eat pumpkin pie on Thanksgiving.
3. The man needed better ______________ on how to assemble the bookcase.
4. Sarah's photograph of her family was her most prized ______________.
5. Kelly's dog, Abby, was her constant ______________ and best friend.
6. The author was sad over the ______________ of his book but hopeful that the next one would be accepted.
7. The ______________ led to a victory for the team.
8. The book had a twist near the end, and Vicki was surprised by the book's

    ______________.

Words Across the Curriculum 

Write the social studies words on the lines.

1. deflation ______________
2. depression ______________
3. inflation ______________
4. recession ______________

Complete the following paragraph with words from above.

Economics

Have you ever heard the word *inflation*? ______________ means a large rise in the price of goods and services. What would be the opposite of inflation? ______________ means the prices of goods and services are falling. You have probably read or heard about the Great ______________. You've probably also heard the word *recession*. A ______________ is a mild depression. These are all terms that explain how the economy works.

NAME ____________________

Lesson 18 Suffixes: **-ion, -tion, -ation**

Words in Writing

Write a letter to a friend about preparing for an event. Use at least five spelling words in your letter.

Using a Dictionary

Write a brief definition for the following spelling words.

1. admiration
2. ambition
3. appreciation
4. companion
5. interception
6. possession
7. production
8. rejection

NAME ______________________

Review Lessons 17–18

Write each of the following spelling words on the lines. Circle the prefixes.

1. disapprove ______________
2. prepaid ______________
3. unlimited ______________
4. disorder ______________
5. preset ______________
6. unsure ______________

Use a dictionary to define the base words and whole words and use them in sentences.

1. definition of base word: ______________
   definition of word with prefix: ______________
   sentence: ______________
2. definition of base word: ______________
   definition of word with prefix: ______________
   sentence: ______________
3. definition of base word: ______________
   definition of word with prefix: ______________
   sentence: ______________
4. definition of base word: ______________
   definition of word with prefix: ______________
   sentence: ______________
5. definition of base word: ______________
   definition of word with prefix: ______________
   sentence: ______________
6. definition of base word: ______________
   definition of word with prefix: ______________
   sentence: ______________

NAME ____________________

Review Lessons 17–18

Write each of the following spelling words on the lines. Circle the suffixes.

1. conclusion ____________________
2. possession ____________________
3. instruction ____________________
4. interception ____________________
5. production ____________________
6. rejection ____________________
7. admiration ____________________
8. appreciation ____________________
9. imagination ____________________
10. preparation ____________________

Complete the following sentences using words from the above list.

1. If the mountain hikers are well prepared, then they have spent much time in ____________________.
2. If the students like to pretend, then they have an active ____________________.
3. If the teacher's efforts are appreciated, then the teacher has received ____________________.
4. If people admire the artists, then the artists have received ____________________.
5. If the application is denied, then the one who has applied has received a ____________________.
6. If the farmer grows many tomatoes, then his ____________________ of tomatoes is large.
7. If the football player is in position to intercept the ball, then there is a good chance the play will result in an ____________________.
8. If the teacher instructs, then what he teaches is his ____________________.
9. If one possesses something, the thing one owns is his or her ____________________.
10. If the speaker concludes his speech with a joke, then the joke is the ____________________.

LESSONS 17–18 REVIEW

NAME ___________________________

Lesson 19 Rhyming Words

Say each of the following words out loud. Then, write each word on the lines.

Spelling Tip	**Rhyming words** are words that have the same sounds at the ends of the word. Even though the spellings may be different, rhymes are made from the same vowel sounds.

Spelling Words

apple ___________________

dapple ___________________

center ___________________

enter ___________________

prince ___________________

mince ___________________

clock ___________________

stock ___________________

bake ___________________

cake ___________________

city ___________________

ditty ___________________

flute ___________________

fruit ___________________

hoot ___________________

NAME ______________________

Lesson 19 Rhyming Words

Fun with Words

Circle all of the spelling words you find in this story. Write the words you circled on the lines below. Underline other pairs of rhyming words that are not spelling words.

This little ditty is about a prince,
A young prince named Prince Vitty.
Prince Vitty lived in a kingdom,
A kingdom within a big city.
Prince Vitty had some favorite things.
Prince Vitty loved a good apple.
He was lucky that his field
Had a bunches of apples.
Prince Vitty also liked to play.
He played a lovely flute.
In his fields, he'd play and hoot
And eat lots of shiny fruit.
Prince Vitty had another love.
Prince Vitty liked to bake.
What do you think his favorite was?
Why it was dapple apple cake.
Prince Vitty was a good baker.
And Prince Vitty played the flute well.
It's too bad he had a job
That made him want to yell.
Prince Vitty couldn't stay outside
He had to watch his clock.
He had to get back to his job,
Which was to watch the stock.
He really didn't like his job,
Which had to do with money.
He would rather play his flute
And sit by a lake that's sunny.
It's not that the prince didn't like to work.
He wanted to earn his keep.
He just had his own ideas
On the rewards he wanted to reap.
One day, his father saw the prince
Return from the lake to enter
The business place of the kingdom
Where stocks and bonds were the center.
Poor Prince Vitty looked so sad,
With thoughts of music and cake,
His father Vince could no longer stand
To continue his terrible mistake.
"Son," his father gently said
And looked him in his eyes.
"I just want you to be happy,
So by night, mince your apples,
And by day, you can bake pies.
Prince Vitty's eyes lit up,
And he hugged his loving father.
"You know there's one who likes the stocks.
It is your only daughter."
Princess Bitty started working
With the kingdom's book
Prince Vitty gladly took the job
Of the city's only flute-playing cook.

______________ ______________ ______________ ______________

______________ ______________ ______________ ______________

______________ ______________ ______________ ______________

______________ ______________ ______________

NAME ____________________

Lesson 19 Rhyming Words

Words Across the Curriculum
Write the sports words on the lines.

1. field ____________________
2. gold ____________________
3. hurdles ____________________
4. track ____________________

Read the following biography. Then, write words from above to answer the questions.

Jackie Joyner-Kersee

Jackie Joyner-Kersee is one of the greatest track and field athletes in sports. Jackie didn't have it easy from the beginning. Her family did not have much money, but they did have spirit. Her parents taught their children to work hard and do their best. Jackie and her brother, Al, spent much of their childhood in the local community center. They exercised and played sports. Track and field became their favorite sport. Jackie excelled at track and field in college. When she was diagnosed with asthma, it made her want to work even harder.

Both Jackie and Al made it to the 1984 Olympic Games. Al earned a gold medal in the triple jump. Jackie earned a silver medal in the heptathlon, an event with seven track and field events, which includes the 100 meter hurdles. Jackie was happy for her brother and pleased with her medal, but she knew she could do better. She practiced harder. In the 1988 Olympic Games, Jackie earned a gold medal in the long jump and in the heptathlon. She set world records in both. She earned her third gold medal in the 1992 Olympic Games. Through hard work, practice, and patience, Jackie Joyner-Kersee succeeded at her goals and lived her dreams.

1. Jackie excelled at the ____________________.
2. Her '88 fate was sealed with two victories in ____________________ and ____________________.
3. Jackie was excited to earn Olympic ____________________ three times.

NAME ____________________

Lesson 19 Rhyming Words

Words in Writing

Write a rhyming poem using at least six words from this lesson. Add rhyming pairs of your own.

____
____
____
____
____
____
____
____
____
____
____
____

Misspelled Words

Complete the following sentences by choosing the correct answer in parentheses. The words in parentheses make the same sound, but only one spelling is correct.

1. When the (clock, clauck) strikes 3:00, school is out.
2. My favorite (caik, cake) is yellow with chocolate icing.
3. Julia lives in the country, and Denise lives in the (city, citee).
4. Peaches are Lyndell's favorite (froot, fruit).
5. Jennifer plays the clarinet, and Lee plays the (flute, floot).
6. Jackie and Al's favorite sport was track and (feeld, field).

NAME ____________________

Lesson 20 Homophones

Say each of the following words out loud. Then, write each word on the lines provided.

Spelling Tip	**Homophones** are words that sound the same but are spelled differently and have different meanings.

Spelling Words

ate ____________________

eight ____________________

beach ____________________

beech ____________________

board ____________________

bored ____________________

feat ____________________

feet ____________________

serf ____________________

surf ____________________

waist ____________________

waste ____________________

pair ____________________

pare ____________________

pear ____________________

NAME ______________________

Lesson 20 Homophones

Words in Context

Complete the following sentences with spelling words. Use a dictionary if you need help.

1. A ______________ tree has dark green leaves, smooth gray bark, and edible nuts.
2. A ______________ is an act of courage, strength, or skill.
3. In the Middle Ages, a ______________ was a farm worker who could be sold along with the property on which he worked.
4. A soft, yellow or green fruit that is round at one end and narrows at the other is a ______________.
5. The past tense of *eat* is ______________.
6. If a speaker is boring, then the audience would surely be ______________.
7. The plural of the word *foot* is ______________.
8. If one would ______________ a pear, he or she would be peeling away the rind.
9. Another word for *trash* is ______________.
10. The waves of the sea breaking on the shore or reef is the ______________.
11. The part of the body between the ribs and the hips is the ______________.
12. A ______________ is a set of two.

Word Building

Write the plural form of the words below.

1. beach ______________
2. beech ______________
3. board ______________
4. feat ______________
5. pear ______________

NAME ___________________________

Lesson 20 Homophones

Words in Context

Read the passage and complete the sentences with spelling words.

Surfing is a fun sport where individuals ride to shore on a breaking wave. Surfers ride on surfboards. A surfer begins at the point where the wave begins to form. Then, the surfer starts paddling toward the beach with the oncoming wave. The surfer stands up when the wave catches the board. The surfer rides the crest of the wave, or if the wave is large, the tube of the wave. You have probably seen the tube in pictures with surfers riding under the overhead curl. Surfing began in Hawaii in the 19th century and spread to California in the 1920s. Hawaii remains a hotspot for surfing.

1. Surfers paddle from the ____________________ out into the sea.
2. To be safe, it's best to surf with a ____________________ of friends.
3. Surfing requires a lot of practice and skill. Surfing is quite a ____________________.

Words Across the Curriculum

Write the music words on the lines beside each word.

1. base ____________________
2. bass ____________________
3. coarse ____________________
4. course ____________________

Complete the following narrative with music words.

Tim wasn't feeling well. His throat felt ____________________. Music is Tim's favorite ____________________. He has a band concert in two days. At least he plays the cymbals, so he can still practice and hopefully be well for the recital.

Tim's best friend, Theo, plays the ____________________ in the band. Tim's favorite sport is baseball. But Theo sprained his ankle running to third ____________________. Fortunately, it wasn't too bad, and Theo can still play with a sprained ankle. Tim and Theo's music teacher, Mr. Anton, is relieved that Tim and Theo can still play. He was starting to think it was a sign that the recital was doomed. However, both Tim and Theo recovered. The recital is a hit!

NAME ______________________

Lesson 20 Homophones

Words in Writing
Write a descriptive narrative using at least six words from this lesson. Make it fun and be creative!

____

____

____

____

____

____

____

____

Using a Dictionary
Hundreds of homophones exist in the English language. Use a dictionary to look up the definitions of each of these pairs of homophones. Write a brief description of each.

1. blew: ______________________

   blue: ______________________
2. creak: ______________________

   creek: ______________________
3. eyelet: ______________________

   islet: ______________________
4. fair: ______________________

   fare: ______________________
5. hair: ______________________

   hare: ______________________
6. might: ______________________

   mite: ______________________
7. principal: ______________________

   principle: ______________________
8. rose: ______________________

   rows: ______________________
9. soar: ______________________

   sore: ______________________
10. toe: ______________________

    tow: ______________________

NAME ______________________

Lesson 21 Easily Confused Words

Say each of the following words out loud. Then, write each word.

Spelling Tip

Some words in the English language are easily confused with other, similar words. Pay careful attention to your writing to make sure you are using the correct word and spelling.

Spelling Words

adapt ______________________

adopt ______________________

accept ______________________

except ______________________

desert ______________________

dessert ______________________

of ______________________

off ______________________

weather ______________________

whether ______________________

were ______________________

where ______________________

breadth ______________________

breath ______________________

breathe ______________________

NAME ____________________

Lesson 21 Easily Confused Words

Words in Context

Complete the following paragraph with spelling words. Not every word will be used. Use a dictionary if you need help.

Hiking the Grand Canyon

Many people enjoy the view of the Grand Canyon in Arizona from the rims above. Its ________________, or expansion of the canyon, is truly amazing. Those who are adventuresome hike down into the canyon below. Much ________________ the lower canyon has a ________________ terrain. The ________________ is hot and dry in the summer and cold and icy in the winter. It is essential to carry plenty of water and food and to wear the appropriate clothing and hiking boots. ________________ you are hiking for just a day or overnight, always consult the authorities for lists of articles to carry.

Many find it difficult to ________________ to the elevation changes. Some people find it hard to ________________. Be prepared for strenuous hiking conditions going into and especially coming out of the canyon. Before departing, ________________ the fact that ________________ conditions can change quickly. It is always best to be prepared for all types of conditions. ________________ a plan for what you want to see, how long you want to be gone, and all of the essentials you need to carry. It is always a good idea to let other people who are not on the trip know ________________ you will be and how long you will be gone.

The sights and sounds of the Grand Canyon can definitely take your ________________ away!

NAME ______________________

Lesson 21 Easily Confused Words

Fun with Words

Complete the following script with spelling words. Some words may be used more than once.

Mom: Riley and Gillian, you can have ________________ after you finish your vegetables. What would you like?

Riley: I would like walnut brownies.

Gillian: I like brownies, ________________ without nuts. Can we have lemon meringue pie?

Riley: I like lemon pie, but can you take the meringue ________________?

Dad: Maybe we can have something else for ________________?

Mom: Alright, how about peach cobbler for ________________, with no nuts and no meringue?

Dad: I think that is something we can all ________________.

Words Across the Curriculum

Write the social studies words on the lines below.

1. emigrate ________________ 2. immigrate ________________

Use a dictionary to define the social studies words. Then, write a sentence using each word.

1. emigrate ____

____

2. immigrate ____

____

NAME ________________

Lesson 21 Easily Confused Words

Words in Writing

Create a comic strip. Write the dialogue in bubbles or in boxes of their own. Draw pictures to go along with the dialogue. Use at least six spelling words.

Words in Context

Circle the best word in each of the following sentences.

1. Ricky is going to (adapt, adopt) a kitten from the local animal shelter.
2. Gianna put all of the fruit in the basket (accept, except) for the bananas that were bad.
3. Mark is going to cross the (desert, dessert) on his trip out West.
4. The runners took (of, off) their jackets when it got warmer.
5. (Were, Where) (were, where) the players going to celebrate their victory?
6. The (weather, whether) was cool and sunny the day of the race.
7. The cave hikers couldn't wait to (breath, breathe) fresh air.
8. It was (decent, descend) of the young man to help the elderly lady with her groceries.

NAME ______________________

Lesson 22 Using a Dictionary

Dictionaries are useful in many ways. Not only can you learn how to spell a word, but you can also learn the origin of the word, its part of speech, and definitions, as well as any alternate spellings. Words are listed alphabetically. The word you are looking up in a dictionary is called the **entry word**.

When you are looking up your entry word, go to the first letter of your word. For example, if you are looking up *proton,* go to the letter **p** first. From there, you can use guide words to help you narrow down the page. **Guide words** are located at the top of each page. The first guide word is the first word on the page. The second guide word is the last word on the page. If the word you are looking up is between the guide words alphabetically, then the word is on that page.

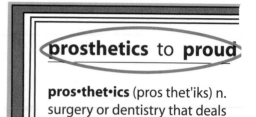

prosthetics to **proud**

pros•thet•ics (pros thet'iks) n. surgery or dentistry that deals with artificial structures. **2.** the fa

Once you have found your entry word on the page, there is a wealth of information about the word. After the entry word, you will see its pronunciation. The pronunciation will help you to pronounce the word if you are unsure. If you are unclear about some of the pronunciation marks used, find the pronunciation key in the dictionary.

unit or cell. 2. a person or thing that is formed first; original; prototype. 3. the hypothetical first individual or species.

pro•to•type (prō'tə tīp), n. v.
1. the original or model on which som

After the pronunciation will be the entry word's part of speech, usually abbreviated, **n.** for *noun,* **v.** for *verb,* **adj.** for *adjective,* or **adv.** for *adverb.* Sometimes, a word has more than one part of speech. All of the parts of speech will be given for an entry word.

The definition of the entry word for each part of speech will be given after the abbreviation of the part of speech. Sometimes more than one definition exists. Each definition will be listed with numbers. Sometimes, example sentences are given along with the definition to help clarify that particular definition.

pro•to•type (prō' tə tīp), n., v. -n **1.** the original or model on which something is based or formed; pattern. **2.** someone that serves as a typical example. -v **3.** to create a prototype.

In addition to the various parts of speech of the entry word, plurals of nouns, tenses of verbs, and comparatives and superlatives of adjectives will also be noted.

Sometimes, even a picture will be given to help illustrate an entry word.

puf • fin (pə-fən), n. any of several sea birds of the genus Fratercula, of the auk family, with a short neck and a colorful, triangular bill.

NAME ____________________

Lesson 22 Using a Dictionary

Write these words in alphabetical order. Then, look them up in the dictionary. Then, write each word, their pronunciations, parts of speech, and definitions on the lines provided.

adventure	**monkey**	**autograph**	**baseball**	**discover**
coach	**chipmunk**	**purple**	**geese**	**imagination**

1. word: ____________________
   pronunciation: ____________________
   part of speech: ____________________
   definition: ____________________
2. word: ____________________
   pronunciation: ____________________
   part of speech: ____________________
   definition: ____________________
3. word: ____________________
   pronunciation: ____________________
   part of speech: ____________________
   definition: ____________________
4. word: ____________________
   pronunciation: ____________________
   part of speech: ____________________
   definition: ____________________
5. word: ____________________
   pronunciation: ____________________
   part of speech: ____________________
   definition: ____________________
6. word: ____________________
   pronunciation: ____________________
   part of speech: ____________________
   definition: ____________________
7. word: ____________________
   pronunciation: ____________________
   part of speech: ____________________
   definition: ____________________
8. word: ____________________
   pronunciation: ____________________
   part of speech: ____________________
   definition: ____________________
9. word: ____________________
   pronunciation: ____________________
   part of speech: ____________________
   definition: ____________________
10. word: ____________________
    pronunciation: ____________________
    part of speech: ____________________
    definition: ____________________

NAME ____________________

Review Lessons 19–22

Write each of the following spelling words on the lines provided.

1. enter ____________
2. center ____________
3. clock ____________
4. stock ____________
5. flute ____________
6. fruit ____________
7. board ____________
8. bored ____________
9. serf ____________
10. surf ____________
11. pare ____________
12. pear ____________

Complete each of the following sentences using words from above.

1. The players jumped for the ball in the ____________ of the court.
2. The group packed nuts, cheese, bread, and ____________ for their lunches.
3. The ____________ of the Middle Ages had a difficult life.
4. The chef used a small knife to ____________ the fruit.
5. The surfer was very particular about the ____________ she used.
6. The ____________ on the wall seemed to tick slower and slower the closer it got to the end of the school day.

NAME ______________________

Review Lessons 19–22

Write each of the following words on the lines.

1. accept ______________
2. except ______________
3. desert ______________
4. dessert ______________
5. were ______________
6. where ______________
7. breath ______________
8. breathe ______________

Complete each of the following sentences using words from above.

1. Becca's class is learning about animals who live in the ______________.
2. After the work out, you should ______________ deeply.
3. Reggie is going to ______________ the invitation to the dance.
4. ______________ is the class going on its next field trip?
5. Strawberry shortcake is Suzie's favorite ______________.
6. After the hard work out, I almost couldn't catch my ______________.
7. Dave likes all vegetables ______________ green peppers.
8. Ricki, Lynne, and Lee ______________ best friends.

NAME ______________________

Review Lessons 19–22

Choose ten words listed from this review lesson and write them in alphabetical order. Then, use a dictionary to write the pronunciations, parts of speech, and definitions.

1. word: ______________________
pronunciation: ______________________
part of speech: ______________________
definition: ______________________

2. word: ______________________
pronunciation: ______________________
part of speech: ______________________
definition: ______________________

3. word: ______________________
pronunciation: ______________________
part of speech: ______________________
definition: ______________________

4. word: ______________________
pronunciation: ______________________
part of speech: ______________________
definition: ______________________

5. word: ______________________
pronunciation: ______________________
part of speech: ______________________
definition: ______________________

6. word: ______________________
pronunciation: ______________________
part of speech: ______________________
definition: ______________________

7. word: ______________________
pronunciation: ______________________
part of speech: ______________________
definition: ______________________

8. word: ______________________
pronunciation: ______________________
part of speech: ______________________
definition: ______________________

9. word: ______________________
pronunciation: ______________________
part of speech: ______________________
definition: ______________________

10. word: ______________________
pronunciation: ______________________
part of speech: ______________________
definition: ______________________

NAME ______________________

Review Lessons 19–22

Choose ten words of your own and write them in alphabetical order. Then, use a dictionary to write the pronunciations, parts of speech, and definitions.

1. word: ______________________

   pronunciation: ______________________

   part of speech: ______________________

   definition: ______________________

2. word: ______________________

   pronunciation: ______________________

   part of speech: ______________________

   definition: ______________________

3. word: ______________________

   pronunciation: ______________________

   part of speech: ______________________

   definition: ______________________

4. word: ______________________

   pronunciation: ______________________

   part of speech: ______________________

   definition: ______________________

5. word: ______________________

   pronunciation: ______________________

   part of speech: ______________________

   definition: ______________________

6. word: ______________________

   pronunciation: ______________________

   part of speech: ______________________

   definition: ______________________

7. word: ______________________

   pronunciation: ______________________

   part of speech: ______________________

   definition: ______________________

8. word: ______________________

   pronunciation: ______________________

   part of speech: ______________________

   definition: ______________________

9. word: ______________________

   pronunciation: ______________________

   part of speech: ______________________

   definition: ______________________

10. word: ______________________

    pronunciation: ______________________

    part of speech: ______________________

    definition: ______________________

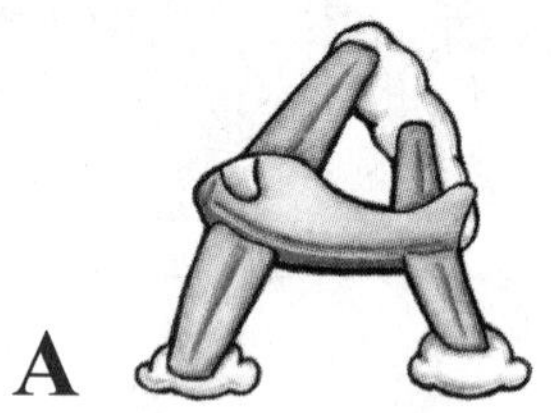

A

ac•cept *v.* To take what is offered or given. ak sept2

ac•ci•dent *n.* An unplanned or unexpected event. ak2 si d@ nt

a•dapt *v.* To fit or suit; to change oneself as to adjust to new conditions. @ dapt2

ad•mi•ra•tion *n.* A feeling of respect and wonder. ad m@ r a$2 sh@ n

a•dopt *v.* To take into one's family legally and raise as one's own; to accept as a process. @ däpt2

ad•ven•ture *n.* An exciting, dangerous, or unusual experience. ad ven2 ch@ r

Af•ri•ca *n.* The second largest continent on Earth. af2 ri k@

af•ter•schock *n.* A tremor after an earthquake. af2 t@ r shäk

air•plane *n.* A fixed-wing vehicle capable of flight, heavier than air, commonly propelled by jet engine or propeller. er2 pla$ n

al•li•ga•tor *n.* Large amphibious reptile with very sharp teeth. al2 @ ga$ t @ r

am•bi•tion *n.* Strong desire to achieve. am bish2 @ n

A•mer•i•can *adj.* Having to do with the United States. @ mer2 @ 2 k@ n

an•i•mals *pl. n.* Beings other than human beings. an2 @ m@ lz

an•noy *v.* To bother; to irritate; to make slightly angry. @ noi2

an•te•lope *n.* An animal similar to a deer. an2 t@ lo$ p

a•part•ment *n.* A suite or room in a building, sharing walls, floor, or ceiling with others, equipped for individual living. @ pärt2 m@ nt

ap•ple *n.* The edible fruit of an apple tree. ap2 @ l

ap•ple•sauce *n.* A sauce made from cooking apples. ap2 @ l sôs

ap•pre•ci•a•tion *n.* The feeling of thanks. @ pre$ she$ a$2 sh@ n

Ar•kan•sas *n.* A state in the United States. är2 k@ n sô

ate *v.* Past tense of *eat.* a$ t

ath•lete *n.* A physically skilled and trained person in sport. ath2 le$ t

a•tri•um *n.* One of the heart chambers; the main hall of a Roman house. a$2 tre$ @ m

aught *pron.* Anything at all. ôt

Au•gust *n.* The eighth month of the year. ô2 gust

au•thor *n.* A person who writes. ô2 th@ r

au•to•graph *n.* A handwritten signature. *v.* To sign with one's signature. ôt2 @ graf

au•tumn *n.* The season between summer and winter. ôt2 @ m

B

bake *v.* To cook in an oven. ba$ k

ban•jo *n.* A stringed instrument similar to a guitar. ban2 jo$

base *n.* One of four corners of a baseball infield. *v.* To begin with. ba$ s

base•ball *n.* A game played with a ball and bat, in which players occupy bases around a diamond; the ball used in a baseball game. ba$ s2 bôl

bass *n.* **1.** A fresh water fish, one of the perch family. bās **2.** A large stringed musical instrument with a deep range. bas

bat•ter•ies *pl. n.* Chemical devices for generating and storing electrical energy. bat′ ər ēz

beach *n.* Pebbly or sandy shore of a lake, ocean, sea, or river. bēch

be•cause *conj.* For a reason; since; from the cause that. bi kôz′

beech *n.* A tree with edible nuts. bēch

bench•es *pl. n.* Long seats for more than two people. bench′ əz

bi•cy•cl•ist *n.* One who rides a bike. bī′ si klist

bi•ol•o•gist *n.* One who studies the life of living things. bī ol′ ə jist

blend *v.* To mix together smoothly. *n.* A mixture of complementary substances. blend

bloom *v.* To bear flowers. blüm

blue•print *n.* A reproduction of technical drawings or plans. blü′ print

board *n.* A flat piece of sawed lumber. bôrd

bo•gus *adj.* Fake. bō′ gəs

book•shelf *n.* An open shelf area used to display and store books. book′ shelf

bored *v.* Past tense of *bore*. To make tired. bôrd

bought *v.* Past tense of *buy*. To purchase. bôt

bowl *n.* A container for food or liquids. bōl

branch *n.* An extension from the main trunk of a tree. branch

breadth *n.* The distance or measurement from side to side. bredth

break *v.* To separate into parts with violence or suddenness. brāk

break•fast *n.* The first meal of the day. brek′ fəst

breath *n.* The air inhaled and exhaled in breathing. breth

breathe *v.* To draw air into and expel from the lungs. brēth

broad *adj.* Covering a wide area. brôd

bro•ken *adj.* Separated violently into parts. brō′ kən

brought *v.* Past tense of *bring*. To carry along with. brôt

bruise *n.* An injury that causes the skin color to darken. brüz

bush•es *pl. n.* Low plants with branches near the ground. boosh′ əz

buzz•es *v.* Making a sound like a bee. buz′ əz

C

cake *n.* A sweet, baked dessert food. kāk

camp *n.* A temporary lodging or makeshift shelter. kamp

can•cel *v.* To stop a procedure or program. kan′ səl

can't *contr.* Short form of *can not*. kant

cap•tain *n.* The chief leader of a group. kap′ tən

caught *v.* Past tense of *catch*. To capture from flight. côt

cau•li•flow•er *n.* A vegetable related to broccoli and cabbage. kôl′ ə flou ər

cen•ter *n.* The place of equal distance from all sides. sen′ tər

cen•tur•ies *pl. n.* Periods consisting of 100 years. sen′ chər ēz

cer•e•brum *n.* The brain structure divided into two cerebral hemispheres and occupying most of the cranial cavity. sə rē′ brəm

chalk *n.* A soft mineral used for marking on a surface. chôk

cham•pi•on *n.* The holder of first place in a contest. cham′ pē ən

char•ac•ter *n.* A trait that distinguishes an individual or group. kər′ ək tər

chest•nut *n.* A tree bearing edible reddish-brown nuts. ches′ nut

chil•dren *pl. n.* Young human beings. chil′ drən

chip•munk *n.* A burrowing striped rodent of the squirrel family. chip′ munk

cit•y *n.* An urban self-governed permanently located community. sit′ ē

clay *n.* A sticky portion of dirt that becomes hard when baked. klā

cli•mate *n.* The weather conditions of a certain region. klī′ mət

climb•er *n.* One who moves to a higher or lower location. klīm′ ər

clock *n.* An instrument that measures time. kläk

coach *n.* A trainer or director of athletics, drama, or other skill. kōch

coarse *adj.* Rough; having large particles. kôrs

cod *n.* A large fish of the North Atlantic. käd

com•pan•ion *n.* An associate; a close friend or fellow traveler. kəm pan′ yən

con•clu•sion *n.* The end. kən klü′ zhən

con•firm *v.* To establish or support the truth of something. kən furm′

con•flict *n.* A battle; clash; a disagreement of ideas, or interests. kän′ flikt

con•ser•va•tion•ist *n.* One who practices protecting something, particularly the environment. kon sər vā′ shə nist

couger *n.* A wild cat. kü′ gər

cough *v.* To suddenly expel air from the lungs with an explosive noise. côf

course *n.* The act of moving in a path from one point to another; a series of studies. kôrs

crawl *v.* To move slowly by dragging the body along the ground in a prone position. krôl

cream *n.* The yellowish, fatty part of milk. krēm

crew *n.* A group of people who work together. krü′

cup•cake *n.* A small baked dessert food. kup′ kāk

cym•bals *n.* Brass instruments that are forced together to make a noise resembling a crash. sim′ bəlz

D

dap•ple *n.* Spotted marking. dap′ əl

da•ta *pl. n.* The numbers or facts of a study or survey. dāt′ ə or dat′ ə

daugh•ter *n.* The female child of a man or woman. dôt′ ər

day•light *n.* The light of day. dā′ līt

de•cent *adj.* Satisfactory; kind; generous. dē′ sənt

deer *n.* A hoofed mammal with antlers. dēr

de•fla•tion *n.* The decrease in consumer prices. dē flā′ shən

de•pres•sion *n.* The state of being or the act of being sad or unhappy; a period of time when the economy is weak. dē presh′ ən

de•scend *v.* To move from a higher to a lower level. dē send′

de•scribe *v.* To tell how something looks or feels; to explain in written or spoken words. də skrīb′

des•ert *n.* A dry, barren region of land without adequate water supply. dez′ ər̸t

des•sert *n.* A serving of sweet foods at the end of a meal. də zurt′

dis•a•gree *v.* To vary in opinion; to differ; to argue. dis ə grē′

dis•ap•point *v.* To fail to satisfy; to let down. dis ə point

dis•ap•prove *v.* To refuse to approve; to reject; to condemn. dis ə prüv′

dis•cov•er *v.* To find for the first time. di skuv′ ər

dis•hon•est *adj.* Lacking honesty. dis än′ əst

dis•or•der *n.* Lack of good order; messiness. dis ôr′ dər

dis•pute *v.* To debate or argue; to question the validity of. di spyūt′

dis•traught *adj.* Deeply worried. di strôt′

dit•ty *n.* A short, simple song. dit′ ē

doc•tor *n.* A person who practices medicine. däk′ tər

don•keys *pl. n.* Animals similar to horses but smaller and with long ears. dôn′ kēz

don't *contr.* Short form of *do not*. dônt

doz•en *n.* Twelve of a kind; a set of twelve things. duz′ ən

draw•bridge *n.* A bridge that can be raised or lowered to allow ships and boats to pass. drô′ brij

drought *n.* A lack of water, usually for a prolonged period of time. drout

E

earth•quake *n.* A sudden movement of Earth's crust, causing violent shaking on the surface of Earth. urth′ kwāk

ech•os *pl. n.* Repetition of sounds by reflecting sound waves from surfaces. ek′ ōz

ed•u•ca•tion *n.* The process of learning. ej ə kā′ shən

eight *n.* The number between seven and nine. āt

e•lec•tric *adj.* Relating to electricity. ē lek′ trik

el•e•phant *n.* A large mammal with thick gray hide and ivory tusks. el′ ə fənt

el•e•va•tions *n.* The height of objects. el′ ə vā shənz

em•i•grate *v.* To move from one country or region to settle elsewhere. em′ ə grāt

emp•ty *adj.* Containing nothing. emp′ tē

en•ter *v.* To go or come into. en′ tər

ex•cept *prep.* With the omission or exclusion of; not including. ek sept′

F

false *adj.* Contrary to truth or fact; incorrect. fôls

feat *n.* A notable act or difficult physical achievement. fēt

feet *pl. n.* The plural of foot. fēt

fern *n.* A plant with spores that grow on the back of its leaves. fərn

field *n.* A piece of land with few or no trees. fēld

fish *n.* A cold-blooded, vertebrated aquatic animal with fins, gills, and usually scales. *v.* To try to catch fish. fish

flash *v.* To burst forth suddenly into a brilliant fire or light; to occur or appear briefly or suddenly. flash

flight *n.* The act or manner of flying. flīt

flute *n.* A high-pitched musical woodwind instrument. flüt

for•est *n.* A large tract of land covered with trees. fôr′ əst

foun•da•tion *n.* The basis on which anything is founded; a fund for helping others. foun dā′ shən

fought *v.* Past tense of fight. fôt

fraught *adj.* Full of or accompanied by something specified. frät

friends *pl. n.* People personally well known and liked. frendz

frost *n.* A light covering of minute ice crystals on a cold surface. frost

fruit *n.* The ripened, mature, seed-bearing part of a flowering plant. früt

fuse *n.* A cord used to carry flame to an explosive devise. fyūz

fu•ture *n.* The time after the present. fyū′ chər

geese *pl. n.* Plural form of *goose*. gēs

gen•er•al *adj.* Common to or typical of most. *n.* Highest ranking military officer. jen′ ər əl

ge•og•ra•phy *n.* The science of the earth's natural climate, resources, and population. jē ôg′ rə fē

gin•ger *n.* A tropical plant used in medicine and cooking as a spice. jin′ jər

gold *n.* A soft, yellow, metallic element used especially in coins and jewelry. gōld

grade *n.* A step or degree in a process or series, a grade in class. grād

grand•fa•ther *n.* The father of one's father or mother. grand′ fä thər

grand•moth•er *n.* The mother of one's father or mother. grand′ muth ər

grand•par•ents *pl. n.* The parents of one's mother or father. grand′ per ənts

grant *v.* To allow; to consent to. *n.* An award of money for a study or experiment. grant

group *n.* A collection or assemblage of people, objects, or things. grüp

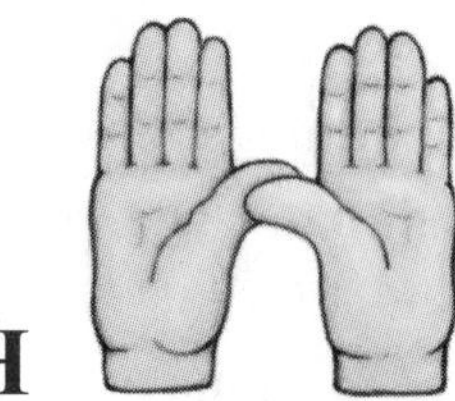

hair•cut *n.* The act of cutting hair. her′ kut

hap•pen *v.* To take place. hap′ ən

he'd *contr.* Short form of he would or he had. hēd

he•roes *pl. n.* people looked up to for bravery. hē′ rōz

hoot *n.* The loud sound or cry of an owl. hüt

horse•back *n.* The back of a horse. *adv.* On the back of a horse. hôrs′ bak

house•work *n.* Work done at a house. hous′ wurk

hur•dles *pl. n.* Portable barriers used to jump over in a race; obstacles one must overcome. hur′ dəlz

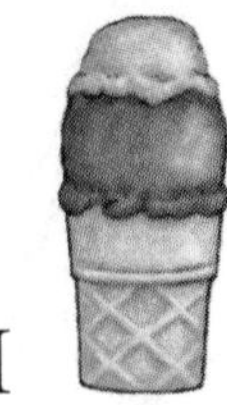

I'll *contr.* Short form of *I will* and *I shall.* īl

I'm *contr.* Short form of *I am.* īm

im•ag•i•na•tion *n.* The power of forming mental images of unreal or absent objects. i maj i nā′ shən

im•mi•grate *v.* To leave one country and settle in another. im′ ə grāt

im•por•tant *adj.* Likely to determine or influence events; significant. im pôr′ tənt

inch *n.* A unit of measurement equal to one twelfth of a foot. *v.* To move slowly. inch

In•di•a *n.* A country in sourthern Asia. in′ dē ə

in•fla•tion *n.* The increase of consumer prices. in flā′ shən

in•side *n.* The part, surface, or space that lies within. in′ sīd

in•struc•tion *n.* The act of teaching. in struk′ shən

in•ter•cep•tion *n.* The interruption of the course of. in tər sept′ shən

in•vent *v.* To design or create by original effort or design. in vent′

I've *contr.* Short form of *I have.* īv

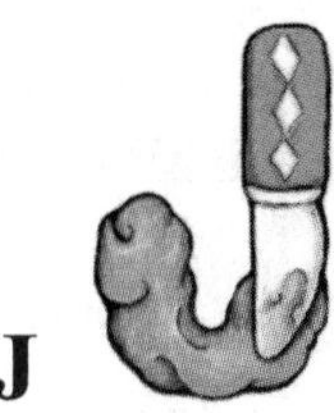

jun•gle *n.* A densely covered land with tropical vegetation, usually inhabited by wild animals. jung′ gəl

kit•ten *n.* A young cat. kit′ n

knap•sack *n.* A supply or equipment bag. nap′ sak

knead *v.* To work dough into a uniform mass by folding over. nēd

knee *n.* The hinged joint in the leg connecting the calf with the thigh. nē

knights *n.* Medieval soldiers serving a monarch. nītz

knock *v.* To hit or strike with a hard blow. näk

knot *n.* An interwinding of string or rope. nät

know *v.* To perceive directly as fact or truth; to believe to be true. nō

la•bel *n.* Something that identifies or describes. lā′ bəl

lawn *n.* A stretch of ground covered with grass mowed regularly. lôn

leg•end *n.* An unverifiable story handed down from the past. lej′ ənd

let's *contr.* Short form of let us. lets

lob•ster *n.* Any of several large marine animals with five pairs of legs. lob′ stər

loy•al *adj.* Faithful in allegiance to one's country and government; faithful to a person, cause, ideal, or custom. loi′ əl

M

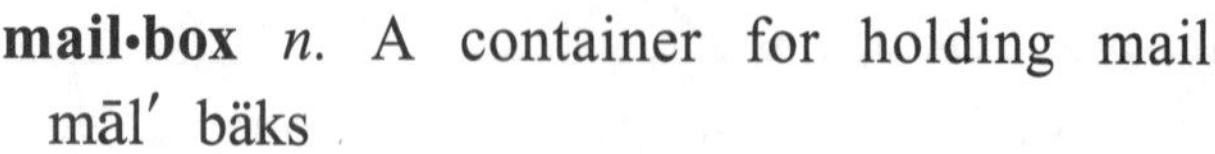

mail•box *n.* A container for holding mail. māl′ bäks

ma•jor *adj.* Greater in importance, quantity, number, or rank; serious. *n.* A military officer. mā′ jər

mar•ket *n.* The trade and commerce in a certain service or commodity; a public place for purchasing and selling merchandise; the possible consumers of a particular product. mär′ kət

med•i•a *pl. n.* The instruments of news communication, as radio, television, and newspapers. mē dē ə

men *pl. n.* Plural form of man. men

me•ter *n.* A unit of measurement equaling 39.37 inches. mēt′ ər

mice *pl. n.* Plural form of mouse. mīs

mile *n.* A unit of measurement equaling 5,280 feet. mīl

mince *v.* To cut or chop something into small pieces. mins

mol•e•cule *n.* The simplest structural unit into which a substance can be divided and still retain its identity. mäl′ ə kyūl

mon•key *n.* A member of the older primates excluding man, having a long-tail. mun′ kē

month *n.* One of the twelve divisions of a calendar year. munth

moose *n.* The largest member of the deer family. müs

N

naught *n.* Nothing; the number 0; zero. nôt

neck•lace *n.* Jewelry worn around the neck. nek′ lis

no•mads *pl. n.* A group of people who wander from place to place. nō′ madz

north•ern *adj.* Having to do with the north. nôr′ thərn

nu•cle•ar *adj.* Relating to atomic energy. nü′ klē ər

nu•cle•us *n.* A central element around which other elements are grouped. nü′ klē əs

numb *adj.* Lacking physical sensation. num

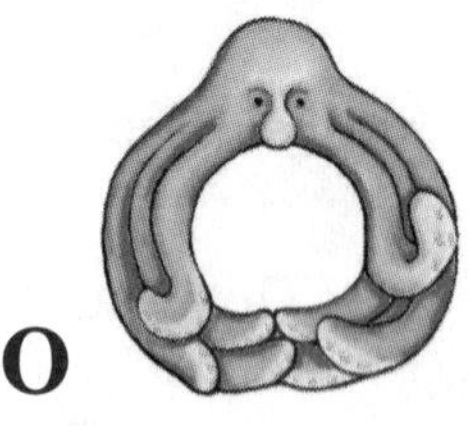

O

ob•ject *v.* To voice disapproval; to protest. *n.* Something visible which can be touched. äb′ jekt

of *prep.* Proceeding; composed of; relating to. uv

off *adv.* From a position or place; no longer connected or on. ôf

of•fi•cers *pl. n.* People who hold a title, position, or office; policemen; military personnel. ôf′ i sərz

ooze *n.* A soft deposit of slimy mud. v. To flow or leak slowly; to disappear little by little. üz

ought *v.* Used to show or express a moral duty or obligation; to be advisable or correct. ôt

our *adj.* Of or relating to us; ourselves. our

out•side *n.* The area beyond the boundary lines or surface. out sīd′

oxen *pl. n.* Plural form of ox. äks′ ən

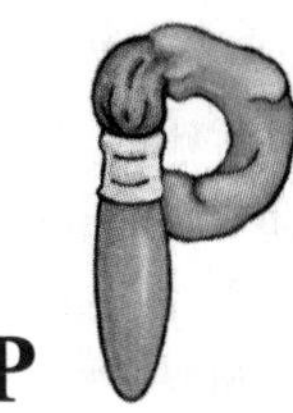

P

pair *n.* Two things similar and used together. per

par•a•chute *n.* A folding umbrella-shaped apparatus of light fabric used to make a safe landing after a free fall from an airplane. per′ ə shüt

pare *v.* To cut away or remove the outer surface gradually. per

pass•es *v.* To proceed; to move; to transfer. pas əz

patch *n.* A piece of fabric used to repair a weakened or torn area in a garment. *v.* To put patches on. pach

pa•ti•os *pl. n.* Areas attached to a house, used for enjoyment and entertainment. pat′ ē ōz

paw *n.* The foot of an animal. pô

pear *n.* A juicy, edible fruit. per

per•haps *adv.* Maybe or possibly. pər haps′

phone *n.* A telephone. fōn

pic•tures *pl. n.* A visual representation printed, drawn, or photographed. pik′ chərz

pi•o•neer *n.* A person who goes before others; one of the first settlers of a new region or country. pī ə nir′

pitch *v.* To throw; to throw out. pich

plumb•er *n.* A person who repairs or installs plumbing in a home or business. plum′ ər

pos•ses•sion *n.* The fact or act of possessing property or an item. pə zesh′ ən

pos•si•ble *adj.* Capable of being true, happening, or being accomplished. pos′ ə bəl

pre•am•ble *n.* An introduction to something, as a law. prē am′ bəl

pre•paid *adj.* Paid before. prē′ pād′

prep•a•ra•tion *n.* The process of preparing for something. prep ər ā′ shən

pre•re•cord•ed *adj.* Recorded before. prē rē kôr′ dəd

pre•school *adj.* Of or for children usually between the ages of two and five. *n.* A school for children between the ages of two and five. prē′ skül

pre•set *adj.* Set before. prē′ set

pre•test *n.* A test before the lesson or activity. prē′ test

prince *n.* The son of a king. prins

prin•ci•pal *n.* The head-master or chief official of a school. prin′ sə pəl

prob•lem *n.* A perplexing situation or question; a question presented for consideration or solution. prob′ ləm

pro•duc•tion *n.* The process or act of producing; something produced, as a play. prə duk′ shən

pro•ton *n.* A unit of positive charge found in the nucleus of an atom. prō′ tän

pub•lish *v.* To print and distribute a book, magazine, or any printed matter to the public. pub′ ish

pur•ple *n.* A color between red and violet. pur′ pəl

R

ra•di•os *pl. n.* Machines that receive radio waves, allowing information to be broadcast. rā′ dē ōz

reach *v.* To stretch out; to be able to grasp. rēch

re•ces•sion *n.* A period or time of reduced economic activity. rē sesh′ ən

re•duce *v.* To decrease; lessen in number, degree, or amount. rē düz′

re•jec•tion *n.* The act of refusing. ri jek′ shən

re•spect *v.* To show consideration or esteem for. rē spekt′

re•turn *v.* To come back to an earlier condition. rē turn′

re•write *v.* To write again. rē rīt′

right tri•an•gle *n.* A triangle with one right (90 degree) angle. rīt trī′ an gəl

risk *v.* To take a chance. *n.* A chance of suffering, harm, or loss. risk

S

salt *n.* A white solid used as a preservative and a seasoning. sôlt

school *n.* A place for teaching and learning. skül

se•cret *n.* Knowledge kept from others; a mystery. sē′ krət

seize *v.* To take forcefully or without consent. sēz

serf *n.* A person who was a slave during the Middle Ages. surf

sheep *n.* A thick-fleeced mammal, related to a goat. shēp

she's *contr.* Short form of she is and she has. shēz

shut•ter *n.* A hinged or swinging cover for a window; a part of a camera that controls the amount of light entering the camera. shut′ər

shut•tle *n.* A vehicle used for space travel; a form of transportation that makes many trips on a short route. shut′ əl

sis•ter *n.* A female having the same parents as another. sis′ tər

skunk *n.* A black mammal with white streaks down its back. skunk

sky *n.* The upper atmosphere above the earth. skī

sleep *n.* The body at a state of rest. *v.* To be in the condition of sleep. slēp

sought *v.* Past tense of seek. To search for an object. sôt

speech *n.* The ability, manner, or act of speaking; a public talk. spēch

spell *v.* To say out loud or write in proper order the letters which make up a word. spel

spin•ach *n.* A widely cultivated plant with dark green leaves, used in salads. spin′ əch

stock *n.* A supply of goods kept on hand. stäk

stom•ach *n.* The organ into which food passes from the esophagus; one of the primary organs of digestion. stum′ ək

straw *n.* A stalk of dried, threshed grain; a slender, plastic or paper straw used to suck up a liquid. strô

stud•y *n.* The process of applying the mind to acquire knowledge. stud′ ē

sub•ject *n.* A person who is under the control of another's governing power; what is being discussed; a course of study. sub′ jekt

sun•set *n.* The time of day the sun goes down. sun′ set

surf *n.* The swell of the sea that breaks upon the shore. *v.* To ride on the crest of a wave on a board. surf

sus•tain *v.* To hold up and keep from falling; to suffer or undergo an injury. sə stān′

sweat•er *n.* A knitted garment. swet′ ər

swung *v.* Past tense of swing. swung

sym•bols *pl. n.* Things that stand for or represents something else. sim′ bəlz

T

taught *v.* Past tense of teach. tôt

tax•es *pl. n.* Payments imposed and collected from individuals or businesses by the government. taks′ əz

teach•ers *pl. n.* People who communicate skills or knowledge. tēch′ ərz

teeth *pl. n.* The plural of tooth. Hard, bone-like structures in the mouth used to chew. tēth

text•book *n.* A book used for class. tekst′ book

that's *contr.* Short form of *that is* and *that has*. thats

thaw *v.* To change from a frozen state to a liquid or soft state. thô

they're *contr.* Short form of *they are*. ther

thirs•ty *adj.* Feeling the need to drink. thurs′ tē

thorn *n.* A sharp point that grows out of a plant stem. thôrn

thought *n.* The process, act, or power of thinking. thôt

thou•sand *n.* The cardinal number equal to 10 x 100. thou′ zənd

to•day *adv.* On or during the present day. *n.* The present time, period, or day. tə dā

to•ma•toes *n.* Garden plants cultivated for their edible fruit; the fruit of such a plant. tə āt′ ōz

tombs *n.* Vaults for burying the dead; graves. tümz

tooth•brush *n.* A tool used for cleaning the teeth. tüth′ brush

tra•che•a *n.* The tube that carries air to the lungs. Also called the *windpipe*. trā′ kē ə

track *n.* A mark, as a footprint, left by the passage of anything; a regular course; a set of rails on which a train runs; a circular or oval course for racing. trak

tra•di•tion *n.* The doctrines, knowledge, practices, and customs passed down from one generation to another. trə dish′ ən

traf•fic *n.* The passage or movement of vehicles. traf′ ik

tri•ceps *n.* Muscles found on the back of the arms, above the elbows. trī′ seps

tro•phy *n.* A prize or object awarded to someone for success. trō′ fē

trough *n.* A container to hold the food and water of animals. trôf

trout *n.* A fish. trout

true *adj.* In accordance with reality or fact. trü

truth *n.* The facts corresponding with actual events or happenings. trüth

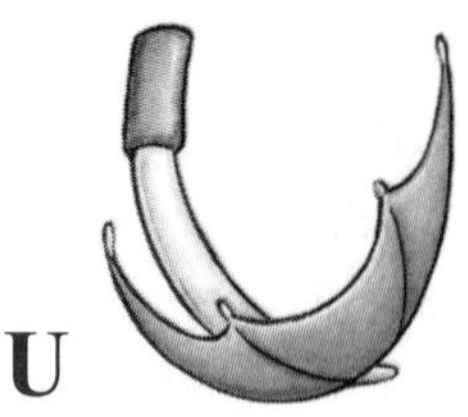

um•brel•la *n.* A collapsible frame covered with plastic or cloth, held above the head as protection from sun or rain. um brel′ ə

un•a•ble *adj.* Not having the capabilities. ən ā′ bəl

un•beat•en *adj.* Having never lost. un bēt′ n

un•cle *n.* The brother of one's mother or father; the husband of one's aunt. un′ kəl

un•clear *adj.* Hard to understand. un klir′

un•der•ground *adj.* Located underneath the surface of the ground. un′ dər ground

un•hap•py *adj.* Sad; without laughter or joy. un hap′ ē

u•ni•form *n.* Identical clothing worn by the members of a group to distinguish them. *adj.* Alike; not different. yū′nə fôrm

un•lim•it•ed *adj.* Having no boundaries. un lim′ it əd

un•sure *adj.* Without confidence. un shür′

un•til *prep.* Up to the time of. un til′

ur•ban *adj.* Pertaining to a city or having characteristics of a city. ur′ bən

va•ca•tion *n.* A period of time away from work for pleasure, relaxation, or rest. vā kā′ shən

val•leys *pl. n.* Low lands between ranges of hills or mountains. val′ ēz

ven•tri•cle *n.* Either of two lower sections of the heart. ven′ tri kəl

Vir•gin•ia *n.* A state on the east coast of the U.S. vər jin′ yə

vol•ley•ball *n.* A sport played on a court with two teams and a net separating them; the ball used in a volleyball game. väl′ ē bôl

voy•age *n.* A long trip or journey. voi′ ij

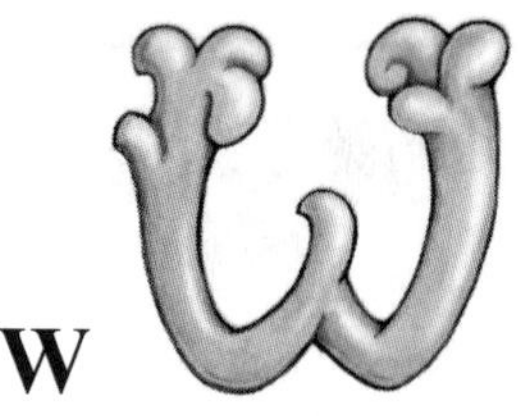

wail *n.* A loud, mournful cry or weep. wāl

wal•nuts *pl. n.* Edible nuts with hard, light-brown shells. wôl′ nuts

watch *v.* To view carefully. *n.* a small timepiece worn on the wrist, designed to keep the correct time of day. wäch

weath•er *n.* The condition of the air or atmosphere in terms of humidity, temperature, and similar features. weth′ ər

weigh *v.* To determine the heaviness of an object by using a scale. wā

were *v.* Past tense of *to be*. wur

weren't *contr.* Short form of *were not*. wurnt

west•ern *adj.* Having to do with the west. wes′ tərn

we've *contr.* Short form of *we have*. wēv

whale *n.* A very large mammal resembling a fish which lives in salt water. hwāl

what's *contr.* Short form of *what is* and *what has*. hwuts

wheat *n.* A grain ground into flour. hwēt

where *adv.* At or in what direction or place. hwer

wheth•er *conj.* Indicating a choice. hweth′ ər

whis•tle *v.* To make a clear shrill sound by blowing air through the mouth. hwis′ əl

width *n.* The distance or extent of something from side to side. width

wo•men *pl. n.* Plural form of *woman.* Mature adult human females. wim′ ən

wouldn't *contr.* Short form of *would not.* wood′ nt

wrap *v.* To conceal an object by covering it. rap

wreath *n.* A decorative ring-like form of intertwined flowers, bows, and other articles. rēth

wren *n.* A small, brown songbird. ren

wres•tle *v.* To struggle with an opponent. res′ əl

wrist *n.* The joint of the body between the hand and forearm. rist

wrong *adj.* Incorrect, not right. rông

Y

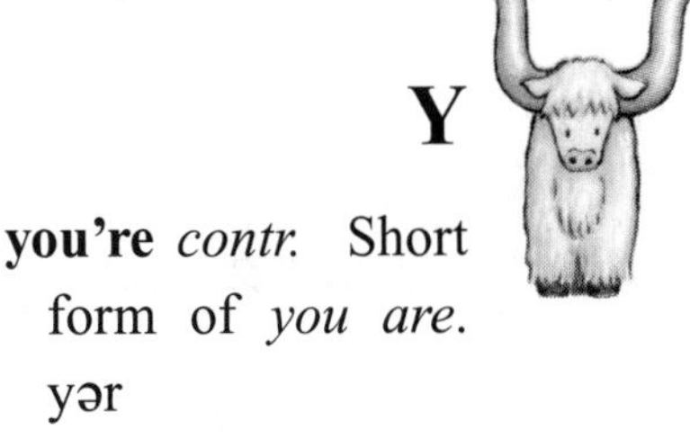

you're *contr.* Short form of *you are.* yər

Parts of Speech

adj. = adjective
adv. = adverb
art. = article
conj. = conjunction
n. = noun
prep. = preposition
pron. = pronoun
v. = verb

Answer Key

Say each of the following words out loud, stressing the short vowel sounds. Then, write the words on the lines provided.

Spelling Tip
Short **a** can be spelled **a**, short **e** can be spelled **e** and **ea**, and short **i** is spelled **i**. The symbol for short **a** is /a/. The symbol for short **e** is /e/. The symbol for short **i** is /i/.

Spelling Words

Word	Answer
perhaps	perhaps
necklace	necklace
sweater	sweater
inch	inch
happen	happen
empty	empty
invent	invent
athlete	athlete
elephant	elephant
until	until
accident	accident
spell	spell
city	city
adventure	adventure
important	important

6

Words in Context
Use the spelling words to fill in the missing blanks. Pay careful attention to the spelling as you write each word in the blank.

Challenge
Circle the other words that have a short **a**, **e**, or **i** sound.

1. Mitzi wore a pretty bracelet and a beautiful **necklace**.
2. I am studying about a big, gray **elephant** in Africa.
3. The **athlete** broke the record for the fastest time.
4. Larry lived in the capital **city**.
5. Sheryl wore a pink **sweater** yesterday.
6. Be careful as you drive so you don't have an **accident**.
7. Who will **invent** the next space tool?
8. Ann can **spell** the best in the class.
9. **Perhaps** we can go to the movies tomorrow night.
10. It measured an **inch** long.
11. Wait **until** tomorrow and we'll go together.
12. Please **empty** the cans before you put them in the bag.
13. What do you think will **happen** at the end of the book?
14. Please sign the **important** papers on your desk.
15. Our trip was quite an **adventure**.

Word Building
Compound words are two words joined together that form a new word. Use the following lines to write as many compound words ... using the word *neck*.

Answers will vary.

7

Fun with Words
Find the 15 spelling words with short **a**, **e**, and **i** vowels in the puzzle below. The words can be forward, backward, horizontal, vertical, and diagonal.

e	p	e	r	h	a	p	s	u	n	t	i	l	e	a
b	l	g	a	t	h	e	l	e	t	e	m	g	b	c
s	w	e	a	t	e	r	m	l	l	e	p	s	i	c
w	q	s	p	m	p	e	u	t	r	i	o	e	b	i
y	y	f	i	h	t	r	n	y	r	r	r	r	e	d
d	t	z	w	e	a	e	j	h	f	y	t	p	m	e
n	i	e	l	l	v	n	e	c	k	l	a	c	e	n
a	c	h	h	n	t	x	t	n	a	o	n	s	d	t
a	t	d	i	k	o	r	y	i	m	d	t	g	a	w
a	d	v	e	n	t	u	r	e	n	e	p	p	a	h

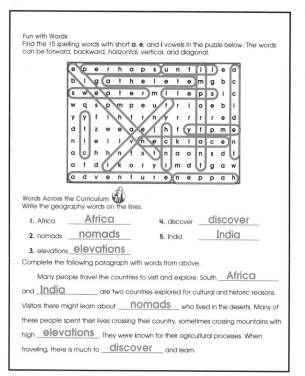

Words Across the Curriculum
Write the geography words on the lines.

1. Africa **Africa**
2. nomads **nomads**
3. elevations **elevations**
4. discover **discover**
5. India **India**

Complete the following paragraph with words from above.

Many people travel the countries to visit and explore. South **Africa** and **India** are two countries explored for cultural and historic reasons. Visitors there might learn about **nomads** who lived in the deserts. Many of these people spent their lives crossing their country, sometimes crossing mountains with high **elevations**. They were known for their agricultural processes. When traveling, there is much to **discover** and learn.

8

Words in Writing
Write a paragraph about a nomadic group of people. Use at least five words from the box.

perhaps	inch	invent	until	city	Africa	discover
necklace	happen	athlete	accident	adventure	nomads	India
sweater	empty	elephant	spell	important	elevations	

Answers will vary.

Misspelled Words
Read the paragraph below. Circle the misspelled words. Write the correct spelling above the misspelled word.

A nomad is a member of a group of people who do not have a stable home. Nomeds (**Nomads**) wander from place to place unitil (**until**) they find food, water, and land to graze their animals. Nomad tribes still live in areas of Africae (**Africa**), Asia, Australia, and the Arctic region. Some nomades (**nomads**) have seasonal homes. These groups of people are seminomadic.

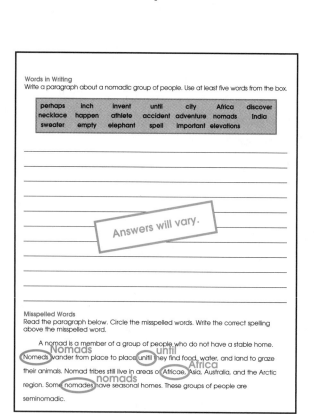

9

Answer Key

Say each of the following words out loud, stressing the short vowel sounds. Then, write the words on the lines.

Spelling Tip

The short **o** sound can be spelled with **o**, **au**, **aw**, **oa**, or **ough**. These letter patterns can have slightly different sounds for short **o**. The symbols for short **o** are /o/ and /ô/. The short **u** sound is spelled with the letter **u**. The symbol for short **u** is /u/.

Spelling Words

possible	possible
because	because
straw	straw
broad	broad
bought	bought
swung	swung
problem	problem
taught	taught
paw	paw
sought	sought
jungle	jungle
brought	brought
shuttle	shuttle
lobster	lobster
umbrella	umbrella

10

Words in Context

Complete the following dialogue using the spelling words. Not all spelling words are used.

Challenge

Circle the other words that have the short **o** or **u** sound.

Maya had brought her special vegetarian pizza for the school cook-off. Now, it looked like Gina had brought the same thing. Because it was a contest, students were not supposed to bring the same recipe. This was a problem. Maya set her pan on the broad food table. Then, she sought her teacher.

"How is this possible?" she asked Mrs. Kaye.

"It's not a problem," answered Mrs. Kaye. "How can we change your recipe?" Mrs. Kaye had always taught her students to think creatively.

"Hmm…," thought Maya. "I know," she blurted. "But it will take me a few minutes."

Fortunately, Maya was early. She found her mother in the auditorium who had bought extra ingredients. First, they spread the tortilla chips in a bowl shaped like an upside down umbrella. Then, they scooped the sauce and vegetables off of the pizza crust and plopped it on the tortilla chips. They sprinkled a little more cheese and added a dab of sour cream. Maya had a new recipe: vegetarian nachos. They were the hit of the cook-off!

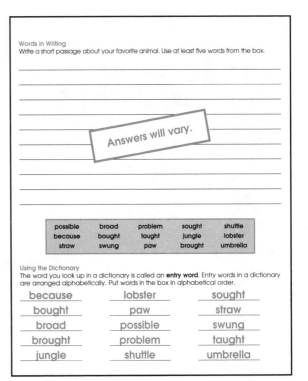

11

Fun with Words

Look at the following pictures. Next to each picture, write a sentence using one of the spelling words from this lesson. Underline the spelling word in your sentence

1.
2.
3.
4. 43 −14 29
5.
6.
7.
8.
9.
10.

Answers will vary.

12

Words in Writing

Write a short passage about your favorite animal. Use at least five words from the box.

Answers will vary.

possible	broad	problem	sought	shuttle
because	bought	taught	jungle	lobster
straw	swung	paw	brought	umbrella

Using the Dictionary

The word you look up in a dictionary is called an **entry word**. Entry words in a dictionary are arranged alphabetically. Put words in the box in alphabetical order.

because	lobster	sought
bought	paw	straw
broad	possible	swung
brought	problem	taught
jungle	shuttle	umbrella

13

Answer Key

Write each of the following words on the lines. Then, circle the letters that make each word have the short **a** or **i** sound.

1. important — important
2. adventure — adventure
3. city — city
4. accident — accident
5. until — until
6. athlete — athlete
7. invent — invent
8. and — and
9. inch — inch
10. nomads — nomads

Write a spelling word that has the short **e** sound that completes each of the following sentences. Then, circle the letter or letters that make this word have the short **e** sound.

1. I can spell all of the words from this list correctly.
2. The elephant is being moved to an animal sanctuary in Tennessee.
3. I was hungry and the box of cereal was empty.
4. My sister wants a new sweater to wear on her birthday.
5. My father got me a sparkling necklace to wear on my birthday.

14

Complete the following paragraph with the spelling words from the box that have the short **o** sound. Then, circle the letter or letters that give the words the short **o** sound.

because	paw	problem	taught
brought	possible	sought	

Henry had a puppy. But the puppy had a problem with his paw. The puppy was Henry's pet and best friend. Henry needed to take care of the puppy because he was the guardian. Henry's teacher had taught his class a lesson on veterinarians. Maybe it was possible he could take his puppy to a vet. He sought out the office on Wilkson Street with his parents and took his puppy there. The doctor said she was glad Henry brought his puppy to the vet. She could make him well again.

Complete the following sentences with spelling words in the box that have the short **u** sound.

jungle	shuttle	swung	umbrella

1. Monkeys live in the jungle.
2. The children swung on the swing set in the park.
3. The students liked learning about the space shuttle in school.
4. Take an umbrella; it looks like it will rain.

15

Say each of the following words out loud, stressing the long vowel sounds. Then, write the words on the lines provided.

Spelling Tip Long **a** can be spelled **a**, **ai**, **ay**, **ea**, **eigh**, and **a-consonant-e**. The symbol for long **a** is /ā/. Long **e** can be spelled **ea**, **ee**, **ei**, **ie**, and **y**. The symbol for long **e** is /ē/. Long **i** can be spelled **i**, **igh**, **y**, and **i-consonent-e**. The symbol for long **i** is /ī/.

Spelling Words

vacation	vacation
reach	reach
describe	describe
sustain	sustain
sleep	sleep
flight	flight
break	break
seize	seize
sky	sky
weigh	weigh
field	field
pioneer	pioneer
airplane	airplane
study	study
clay	clay

16

Words in Context

Complete the following paragraph using the spelling words. Not every spelling word is used.

Wilbur and Orville Wright

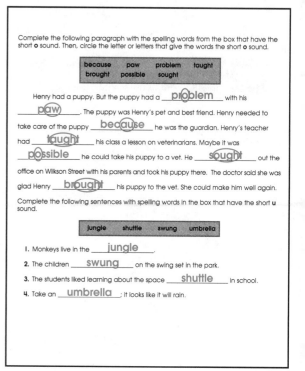

How would you describe a pioneer? A pioneer is not just a person who crossed a corn field of America in the old west. A pioneer is someone who opens the way for others. Who opened the way to the sky? The Wright brothers did. Orville and Wilbur Wright were born in Dayton, Ohio in the mid-1800s. In 1903, near Kitty Hawk, North Carolina, the Wright brothers made the first sustained flight in a power-driven airplane. The Wright brothers continued to make several flying records. A great vacation would be to visit the Wright Brothers National Memorial in Kill Devil Hills, North Carolina.

Word Building

The spelling words below are verbs. Regular present tense verbs are made into past tense by adding **ed**. Write the four spelling words on the lines. Then, write the past tense form of these verbs on the lines beside them. If a verb ends in the letter **y**, change the **y** to **i** and then add **ed**.

reach	reach	reached
seize	seize	seized
weigh	weigh	weighed
study	study	studied

17

Answer Key

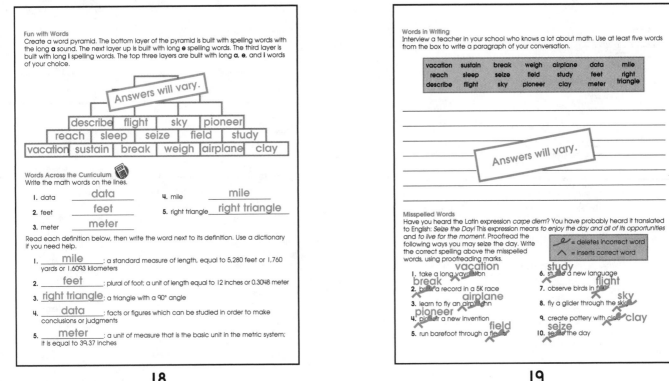

Fun with Words
Create a word pyramid. The bottom layer of the pyramid is built with spelling words with the long **a** sound. The next layer up is built with long **e** spelling words. The third layer is built with long **i** spelling words. The top three layers are built with long **a**, **e**, and **i** words of your choice.

Answers will vary.

describe	flight	sky	pioneer		
reach	sleep	seize	field	study	
vacation	sustain	break	weigh	airplane	clay

Words Across the Curriculum
Write the math words on the lines.

1. data — data
2. feet — feet
3. meter — meter
4. mile — mile
5. right triangle — right triangle

Read each definition below, then write the word next to its definition. Use a dictionary if you need help.

1. mile: a standard measure of length, equal to 5,280 feet or 1,760 yards or 1.6093 kilometers
2. feet: plural of foot; a unit of length equal to 12 inches or 0.3048 meter
3. right triangle: a triangle with a 90° angle
4. data: facts or figures which can be studied in order to make conclusions or judgments
5. meter: a unit of measure that is the basic unit in the metric system; it is equal to 39.37 inches

18

Words in Writing
Interview a teacher in your school who knows a lot about math. Use at least five words from the box to write a paragraph of your conversation.

vacation	sustain	break	weigh	airplane	data	mile
reach	sleep	seize	field	study	feet	right triangle
describe	flight	sky	pioneer	clay	meter	

Answers will vary.

Misspelled Words
Have you heard the Latin expression *carpe diem*? You have probably heard it translated to English: *Seize the Day!* This expression means *to enjoy the day and all of its opportunities* and *to live for the moment*. Proofread the following ways you may seize the day. Write the correct spelling above the misspelled words, using proofreading marks.

= deletes incorrect word
= inserts correct word

1. take a long vacation
2. break a record in a 5K race
3. learn to fly an airplane
4. pioneer a new invention
5. run barefoot through a field
6. study a new language
7. observe birds in flight
8. fly a glider through the sky
9. create pottery with clay
10. seize the day

19

Say each of the following words out loud, stressing the long vowel sounds. Then, write the words on the lines provided. Over emphasize the difference between the /ū/ and the /ü/.

Spelling Tip Long **o** can be spelled **o**, **oa**, **ow**, and **o-consonant-e**. The symbol for long **o** is /ō/. Long **u** has two sounds. The /ū/ sound can be spelled **u** and has a /y/ sound at the beginning of the vowel. The /ü/ sound can be spelled **u**, **ue**, **ew**, **oo**, **ou**, **u-consonant-e**, and **ui-consonant-e**. The difference between /ū/ and /ü/ is slight.

Spelling Words

bogus	bogus
uniform	uniform
coach	coach
truth	truth
bowl	bowl
true	true
antelope	antelope
crew	crew
school	school
group	group
parachute	parachute
bruise	bruise
future	future
ooze	ooze
reduce	reduce

20

Words in Context
Complete the following sentences using spelling words

1. Monica liked her new band uniform.
2. There was red ooze coming out of Mark's volcano science experiment.
3. The soccer coach announced that practice would begin right after school.
4. The future is yet to be known.
5. Jerry likes a big bowl of cereal for breakfast.
6. Kyoko got a bruise on her knee when she fell off of her bike.
7. The parachute opened right on time.
8. The antelope is related to the oxen and the goat.
9. The whole group of students enjoyed the field trip.
10. The crew of the space shuttle was excited for the trip.
11. Abraham participated in many school activities.
12. The teacher asked a series of true or false questions.
13. Don't spend the monopoly money; it is bogus money.
14. I will not lie; I will always tell the truth.
15. Put ice on your bruised knee to help reduce the swelling.

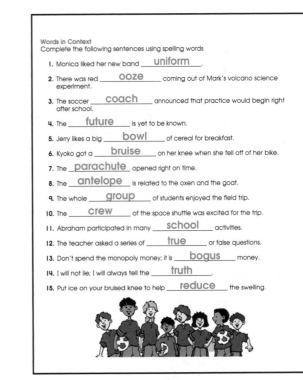

21

Answer Key

Fun with Words

Read the following sentences. After each question, write whether the sentence is **true** or **false**. Then, circle the spelling word or words found in the sentence.

1. A parachute is used to slow down a person dropping from an airplane. — true
2. You wouldn't find a coach in a school. — false
3. Antelope are related to oxen and goats. — true
4. If you drop an apple, it might bruise. — true
5. If you reduce the number in a group, then you will have more. — false
6. One might find ooze on the trunk of a maple tree. — true
7. A one-man team is called a crew. — false
8. The future is a time in the past. — false

Words Across the Curriculum

Write the following science words on the lines.

1. fuse — fuse
2. molecule — molecule
3. nuclear — nuclear
4. nucleus — nucleus
5. proton — proton

Write the science word next to its definition. Use a dictionary if you need help.

1. proton: This particle has a single, electric charge. It is part of the nucleus of an atom.
2. fuse: The verb form of this word means *to unite* or to *join together by melting*.
3. nucleus: This is the center part of the atom.
4. nuclear: This adjective involves the use of the nuclei of atoms.
5. molecule: This is the smallest particle of a substance that can exist alone without losing its chemical form.

22

Words in Writing

Write a letter to a friend using at least five spelling words.

Answers will vary.

Using the Dictionary

The sound difference between the /ü/ and the /ū/ spellings can seem quite slight. However, when you pronounce the words, you can hear a difference. The vowel sounds in the following pronunciations are missing. Add the correct symbol for the sound. Then, write the word.

/ü/ = ōō
/ū/ = yōō

1. brüz — bruise
2. krü — crew
3. fū′ cher — future
4. grüp — group
5. üz — ooze
6. per′ ə shüt — parachute
7. rē düs′ — reduce
8. sküI — school
9. trü — true
10. trüth — truth
11. ū′n′ ə fôrm — uniform
12. fūz — fuse
13. mäl′ ə kūI — molecule
14. nü′ klē ər — nuclear
15. nü′ klē əs — nucleus

23

Write each of the spelling words below. Then, circle the letter or letters that make each word have the long **a**, **e**, or **i** sound.

1. sustain — sustain
2. way — way
3. break — break
4. weigh — weigh
5. reach — reach
6. pioneer — pioneer
7. seize — seize
8. field — field
9. flight — flight
10. sky — sky

Write a word from Lesson 3 that has the long **a**, **e**, or **i** sound that completes each of the following sentences.

1. Are you going to take a vacation this spring break?
2. Melissa is hoping to break the long jump record.
3. The airplane is delayed and won't arrive for another hour.
4. Michael found out his great-great-grandmother was a pioneer.
5. Leigh and Bob love to climb mountains.
6. The sky is really blue today.
7. The trucks have to pass through the weigh stations on the freeway.
8. The lost and found officer asked Sandra to describe the missing bracelet.
9. The farmers plowed the field and prepared for the following day's work.
10. The birds' flight patterns are amazing to watch.

24

Write each of the following spelling words. Then, circle the letter or letters that make each word have the long **o** or long **u** sound.

1. coach — coach
2. bowl — bowl
3. antelope — antelope
4. uniform — uniform
5. true — true
6. crew — crew
7. school — school
8. group — group
9. parachute — parachute
10. bruise — bruise

Complete the following paragraph with the spelling words from Lesson 4 that have the long **o** or **u** sound. Then, circle other words in the paragraph with a long **o** or **u** sound.

The team was ready. It was a beautiful day. The members of the crew had been practicing for months and in all types of weather. The coach was proud of her team. It was a slow start. Many girls dropped out. The uniforms weren't ready for the first meet. One girl suffered a serious bruise and had to take several weeks off. The weather wasn't cooperating either. But now, the school was in the semifinals. One more regatta, a boat race, and the group would advance to the finals. Today was this team's day. Today, the truth would be known. They were ready!

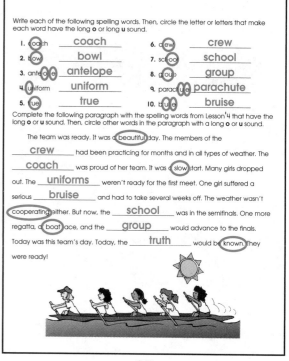

25

Answer Key

Say the following words out loud. Then, write each one on the lines provided.

Spelling Tip	The /j/ sound can be spelled with **j** or **g**. The /k/ sound can be spelled with **k**, **c**, or **ch**.

Spelling Words

banjo	banjo
broken	broken
general	general
American	American
major	major
kitten	kitten
ginger	ginger
camp	camp
object	object
market	market
legend	legend
character	character
subject	subject
monkey	monkey
electric	electric

26

Words in Context
Use spelling words to complete the paragraph. Not every word is used.

Challenge
Circle other words with the /j/ and /k/ sounds.

Sullivan Ballou

Have you ever heard of (Major) Sullivan Ballou? He may not be a famous legend of the American Civil War, but he should definitely be remembered. Ballou was a strong supporter of President Abraham (Lincoln). He decided to enlist in the Union Army and serve under General Ulysses S. Grant. Major Sullivan Ballou was stationed at (Camp Clark), a camp near Washington, D.C. Ballou did not have a good feeling about the upcoming battle. Though his spirits were not broken, he did not believe he would survive the war. At (Camp Clark), he wrote a letter to his wife. The subject was his love for her and their children, his passion for the Union Army, and his worries about dying in battle. Fifteen days later, at the First Battle of Bull Run, (Major) Ballou and many of his men were (killed). Altogether, four thousand (Americans) lost their lives at this battle. (Major) Ballou's letter is now published. You (can) learn more about this brave soldier with (remarkable) character by reading his letter.

Word Building
Synonyms are words that have the same or similar meaning. Write the spelling word that is a synonym of each word below.

1. famous legend
2. dynamic electric
3. item object
4. shattered broken
5. shelter camp
6. store market

27

Fun with Words
Complete the puzzle using spelling words.

Across
1. The _____ light went out during the storm.
3. You can pick up fruit and vegetables at the _____.
5. A _____ is a stringed musical instrument.
7. The _____ of the game *Jeopardy* is to provide the questions to given answers.

Down
2. You can adopt a dog, puppy, cat, or _____, from an animal shelter.
3. A _____ lives in a jungle.
4. Social studies is one _____ in school.
6. _____ is a spice made from the root of a plant.

												[2]k	
						[1]e	l	e	c	t	r	i	c
												t	
					[4]s		[3]m	a	r	k	e	t	
					u		o					e	
			[6]g		[5]b	a	n	j	o			n	
			i		j		k						
			n		e		e						
			g		c		y						
[7]o	b	j	e	c	t								
			r										

Words Across the Curriculum
Write the social studies words on the lines.

1. captain captain
2. climate climate
3. crew crew
4. geography geography
5. voyage voyage

Complete the following sentences with social studies words.

1. Captain James Cook was an explorer who commanded the ship, *Endeavor*.
2. He and his crew set sail in 1768.
3. Their voyage circumnavigated the globe.
4. On his second trip, he explored the cold climate of the Antarctic Ocean.
5. During his third trip, Cook tested his knowledge of geography to find the Northwest passage.

28

Words in Writing
Write a biography about a famous figure from history. Use at least five words from the box.

banjo	American	ginger	market	subject	captain	geography
broken	major	camp	legend	monkey	climate	voyage
general	kitten	object	character	electric	crew	

Answers will vary.

Misspelled Words
Circle the misspelled words in each sentence and rewrite them correctly.

1. Stacy played her (bango) all evening. banjo
2. The (jeneral) was respected by his troops. general
3. Thomas played a (magor) role in winning the baseball game. major
4. I like to sprinkle (ginjer) on my vanilla pudding. ginger
5. Bill loves to go to summer (kamp). camp
6. Mom goes to the (marcet) every Saturday morning. market
7. I have to think of one more (charakter) for the skit I'm writing. character
8. Jane Goodall was given a toy (moncey) when she was a little girl. monkey
9. Doug will be the (kaptain) of our football team. captain
10. I prefer a warmer (klimate). climate

29

Answer Key

30

Say each word out loud. Then, write each word.

Spelling Tip — **Consonant digraphs** are two or more consonant letters that together make one specific sound.

Spelling Words

chestnut	chestnut
trophy	trophy
shutter	shutter
thorn	thorn
pitch	pitch
whale	whale
chipmunk	chipmunk
phone	phone
toothbrush	toothbrush
month	month
patch	patch
whistle	whistle
speech	speech
width	width
watch	watch

31

Words in Context
Complete the following story with spelling words.

It had been three hours since I had received the phone call. Mom had asked that I watch the tea kettle and turn it off when it began to whistle. I was putting away my toothbrush when the water began to boil in the kettle. I turned it off and turned around just as the phone rang. I answered, and the woman on the other end said, "It's time."

I had a speech ready for just this occasion, but all I could do was squeak like a little chipmunk. I asked her when I needed to be ready, figuring it would be a week or a month. "Three hours," she replied.

I quickly hung up the phone, ran the width of the room to get my stuff, closed the shutter on the front window, and locked the front door behind me. Mom was working in the garden when I told her where I was going. That was three hours ago.

The chestnut trees swayed in the wind. A cloud as big as a whale floated above me. I stood on a patch of dirt in the center of the field. I still couldn't believe I was called up to pitch. I was nervous when I threw the first pitch. It felt like a thorn was poking me. But after nine innings, I brought home a trophy from my first little league baseball start.

32

Fun with Words
Look at the following pictures. Next to each picture, write a sentence using the spelling word that names the picture. Underline the spelling word in your sentence.

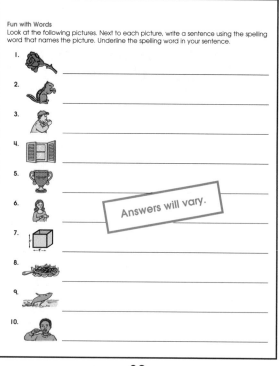

1.
2.
3.
4.
5.
6.
7.
8.
9.
10.

Answers will vary.

33

Words in Writing
Write a fictional dialogue between at least three characters about a sporting event. Use at least five words from the box.

chestnut	thorn	chipmunk	month	speech
trophy	pitch	phone	patch	width
shutter	whale	toothbrush	whistle	watch

Answers will vary.

Using the Dictionary
Look up each spelling word in a dictionary and write the parts of speech listed.

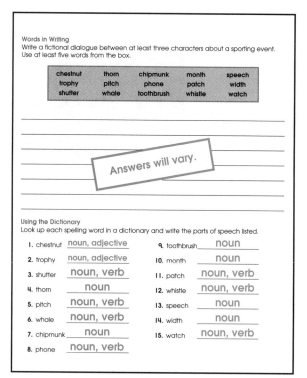

1. chestnut noun, adjective
2. trophy noun, adjective
3. shutter noun, verb
4. thorn noun
5. pitch noun, verb
6. whale noun, verb
7. chipmunk noun
8. phone noun, verb
9. toothbrush noun
10. month noun
11. patch noun, verb
12. whistle noun, verb
13. speech noun
14. width noun
15. watch noun, verb

Answer Key

Say each word out loud. Then, write each word on the lines provided.

Spelling Tip	**Consonant blends** are two or more consonant letters that run together. Each letter is still heard.

Spelling Words

blend	blend
conflict	conflict
branch	branch
cream	cream
grant	grant
risk	risk
respect	respect
frost	frost
bloom	bloom
flash	flash
breakfast	breakfast
secret	secret
grade	grade
skunk	skunk
spinach	spinach

34

Words in Context
Complete each sentence with spelling words.

1. Spinach is a very good food for you to eat.
2. Don't forget to blend the strawberries and bananas together.
3. I think I see and smell a skunk over in the trees.
4. The class had a conflict over which book to read.
5. The teacher will grade the papers this weekend.
6. The tree branch looks small compared to the big tree.
7. Stacy promised not to tell her best friend's secret.
8. Do you like cream in your coffee?
9. Grace likes pancakes with syrup for breakfast.
10. The teacher said she would grant a reading request from each student.
11. The lightning was like a flash in the sky.
12. Bridget took a risk and attempted to run the whole distance.
13. The flowers will bloom in the spring.
14. The students had a lot of respect for their teacher.
15. The frost came early this fall.

Word Building
Antonyms are words that have the opposite or close to the opposite meanings of each other. Write the spelling words that are the antonyms of the words below.

1. separate blend
2. agreement conflict
3. refuse grant
4. safe risk
5. scorn respect

35

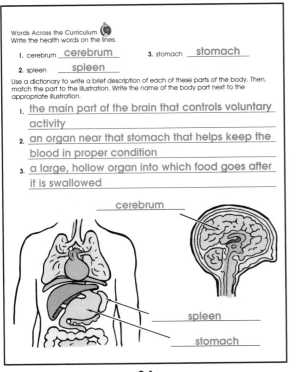

Words Across the Curriculum
Write the health words on the lines.

1. cerebrum cerebrum
2. spleen spleen
3. stomach stomach

Use a dictionary to write a brief description of each of these parts of the body. Then, match the part to the illustration. Write the name of the body part next to the appropriate illustration.

1. the main part of the brain that controls voluntary activity
2. an organ near that stomach that helps keep the blood in proper condition
3. a large, hollow organ into which food goes after it is swallowed

cerebrum

spleen

stomach

36

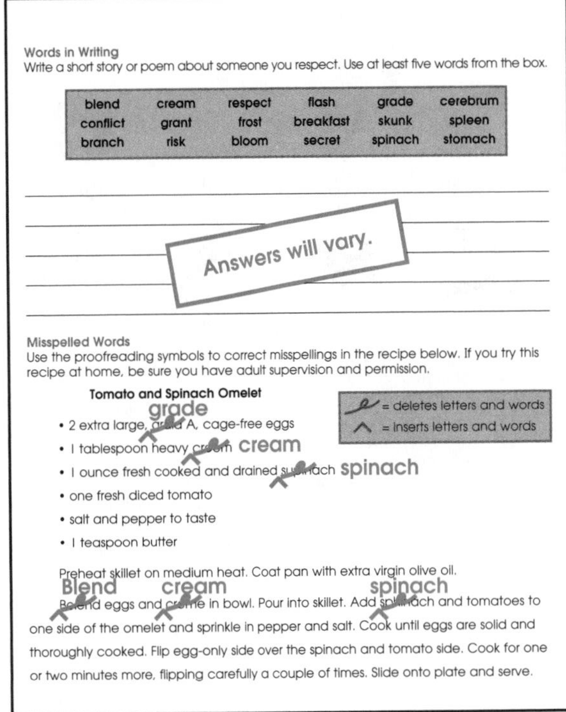

Words in Writing
Write a short story or poem about someone you respect. Use at least five words from the box.

blend	cream	respect	flash	grade	cerebrum
conflict	grant	frost	breakfast	skunk	spleen
branch	risk	bloom	secret	spinach	stomach

Answers will vary.

Misspelled Words
Use the proofreading symbols to correct misspellings in the recipe below. If you try this recipe at home, be sure you have adult supervision and permission.

= deletes letters and words
^ = inserts letters and words

Tomato and Spinach Omelet

- 2 extra large, grade A, cage-free eggs
- 1 tablespoon heavy cream
- 1 ounce fresh cooked and drained spinach
- one fresh diced tomato
- salt and pepper to taste
- 1 teaspoon butter

Preheat skillet on medium heat. Coat pan with extra virgin olive oil. Blend eggs and cream in bowl. Pour into skillet. Add spinach and tomatoes to one side of the omelet and sprinkle in pepper and salt. Cook until eggs are solid and thoroughly cooked. Flip egg-only side over the spinach and tomato side. Cook for one or two minutes more, flipping carefully a couple of times. Slide onto plate and serve.

37

Answer Key

Say each word out loud. Then, write each word on the line.

Spelling Tip: Some consonant combinations produce silent letters. In the consonant combination **kn**, only the **n** is pronounced. In **mb**, only the **m** is pronounced, and in **wr**, only the **r** is pronounced.

Spelling Words

knapsack	knapsack
rewrite	rewrite
knead	knead
climber	climber
wreath	wreath
knee	knee
wren	wren
knock	knock
numb	numb
wrestle	wrestle
knot	knot
wrist	wrist
know	know
plumber	plumber
wrong	wrong

38

Words in Context

Complete the following paragraph with spelling words. Not every word will be used.

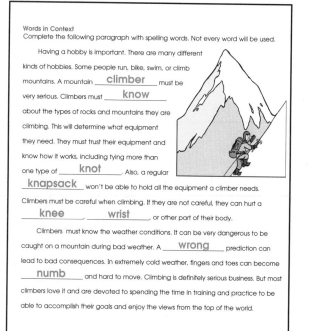

Having a hobby is important. There are many different kinds of hobbies. Some people run, bike, swim, or climb mountains. A mountain climber must be very serious. Climbers must know about the types of rocks and mountains they are climbing. This will determine what equipment they need. They must trust their equipment and know how it works, including tying more than one type of knot. Also, a regular knapsack won't be able to hold all the equipment a climber needs. Climbers must be careful when climbing. If they are not careful, they can hurt a knee, wrist, or other part of their body.

Climbers must know the weather conditions. It can be very dangerous to be caught on a mountain during bad weather. A wrong prediction can lead to bad consequences. In extremely cold weather, fingers and toes can become numb and hard to move. Climbing is definitely serious business. But most climbers love it and are devoted to spending the time in training and practice to be able to accomplish their goals and enjoy the views from the top of the world.

39

Fun with Words

Write the spelling word that each picture represents.

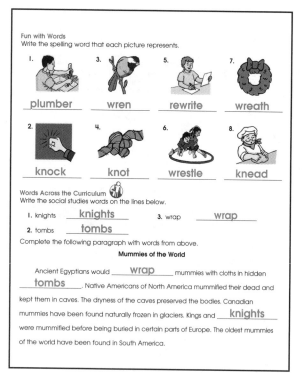

1. plumber
2. knock
3. wren
4. knot
5. rewrite
6. wrestle
7. wreath
8. knead

Words Across the Curriculum

Write the social studies words on the lines below.

1. knights knights
2. tombs tombs
3. wrap wrap

Complete the following paragraph with words from above.

Mummies of the World

Ancient Egyptians would wrap mummies with cloths in hidden tombs. Native Americans of North America mummified their dead and kept them in caves. The dryness of the caves preserved the bodies. Canadian mummies have been found naturally frozen in glaciers. Kings and knights were mummified before being buried in certain parts of Europe. The oldest mummies of the world have been found in South America.

40

Words in Writing

Write a paragraph describing your favorite hobby. Include at least five words from the box.

knapsack	climber	wren	wrestle	know	knights
rewrite	wreath	knock	knot	plumber	tombs
knead	knee	numb	wrist	wrong	wrap

Answers will vary.

Using the Dictionary

Look up the pronunciations of the following spelling words and write them on the lines provided. Notice that the **k** in **kn** words, the **b** in **mb** words, and the **w** in **wr** words are not given in the pronunciation, since they are silent.

1. knapsack nap′ sak
2. rewrite rē rīt′
3. knead nēd
4. climber klīm′ ər
5. wreath rēth
6. knee nē
7. wren ren
8. knock näk
9. numb num
10. wrestle res′ əl
11. knot nät
12. wrist rist
13. know nō
14. plumber plum′ ər
15. wrong rông
16. knights nītz
17. tombs tümz
18. wrap rap

41

Answer Key

Write each of the following words. Circle the consonant sounds /j/ and /k/. Underline the consonant digraphs.

1. banjo — banjo
2. monkey — monkey
3. watch — watch
4. electric — electric
5. thorn — thorn
6. trophy — trophy
7. general — general
8. toothbrush — toothbrush
9. whale — whale
10. chipmunk — chipmunk

Write a word from Lesson 5 or 6 that completes each of the following sentences.

1. My sister is going to major in communication in college.
2. Anna's favorite cookies are ginger snaps.
3. Jill adopted a kitten from the humane society.
4. Sam is my favorite character in *The Lord of the Rings.*
5. Donna is going to give a speech in her political science class.
6. A cell phone can come in very handy in emergencies.
7. The shutter made a loud noise when the wind blew it closed.
8. Be sure to measure both the height and the width of the box before shipping.
9. The coach blows his whistle when he is ready to start practice.
10. Who is going to throw the first pitch at the game?

42

Write each of the following words. Circle the consonant blends. Underline the silent letter combinations.

1. blend — blend
2. flash — flash
3. branch — branch
4. cream — cream
5. grant — grant
6. wrestle — wrestle
7. skunk — skunk
8. respect — respect
9. frost — frost
10. knead — knead
11. climber — climber
12. breakfast — breakfast

Complete the following sentences by filling in the blanks with words from Lesson 7 or 8.

1. A wren is a small songbird with a narrow bill and a stubby tail that tilts up.
2. A good morning breakfast for these birds would be insects and fruit.
3. The flight of these birds can be quick and irregular.
4. These birds can use their slender bills to investigate a crevice.
5. They nest in cavities, like birdhouses and nests built out of a tree branch and grass.
6. A wreath on a door has become the home of some nests.
7. If you know the sound these songbirds make in your area, you might be able to identify them.

43

Say each word out loud. Then, write each word on the lines provided.

Spelling Tip
Some vowel combinations make special sounds. The /al/, /au/, and /aw/ sounds make the short **o** sound, as in the word *dog.* It is a slightly longer sound than some other short **o** words. The /ou/ and /oy/ sounds make the vowel sound in *shower.* **Dipthongs** are vowel combinations that make a new sound. The /au/, /aw/, /ou/, /oy/ sounds are dipthongs. The schwa sound is an unaccented vowel followed by an **l** (or other consonant).

Spelling Words

chalk	chalk
August	August
crawl	crawl
foundation	foundation
annoy	annoy
cancel	cancel
false	false
author	author
lawn	lawn
our	our
loyal	loyal
label	label
salt	salt
autograph	autograph
outside	outside

44

Words in Context
Write a spelling word to complete the following sentences.

1. The movie star signed an autograph as he left the theater.
2. After all of the rain, the lawn looked nice and green.
3. Since it stopped raining, the students played outside during recess.
4. The best friends had been loyal to each other for years.
5. The teacher used different colored chalk to write the assignment on the board.
6. The coaches might have to cancel the game if it doesn't stop raining soon.
7. The foundation raises money for patients in the hospital.
8. Our teacher said to put a label on our books so they won't get mixed up.
9. The baby is learning to crawl across the floor.
10. The author has written many good books.

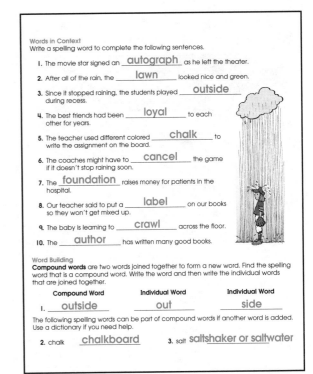

Word Building
Compound words are two words joined together to form a new word. Find the spelling word that is a compound word. Write the word and then write the individual words that are joined together.

	Compound Word	Individual Word	Individual Word
1.	outside	out	side

The following spelling words can be part of compound words if another word is added. Use a dictionary if you need help.

2. chalk chalkboard
3. salt saltshaker or saltwater

45

Answer Key

Fun with Words
Unscramble the spelling words in the following sentences.

1. The magazine publisher said, "We are yolal **loyal** to our ouraht **author** even though he sometimes will nonya **annoy** the readers."
2. The chef said, "If you add tlas **salt** to the sauce, it will alter the flavor."
3. The weather reporter said, "It was a lfesa **false** report that the storm struck in gsuutA **August**."
4. The mother said, "We are so proud, because rou **our** baby can waclr **crawl** across the entire wain **lawn**."
5. The director said, "The onainfudaot **foundation** must nclace **cancel** the event in guAstu **August** and move it to September."

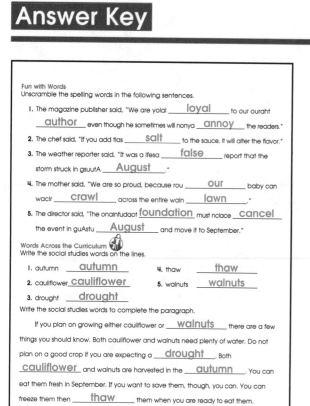

Words Across the Curriculum
Write the social studies words on the lines.

1. autumn **autumn**
2. cauliflower **cauliflower**
3. drought **drought**
4. thaw **thaw**
5. walnuts **walnuts**

Write the social studies words to complete the paragraph.

If you plan on growing either cauliflower or **walnuts** there are a few things you should know. Both cauliflower and walnuts need plenty of water. Do not plan on a good crop if you are expecting a **drought**. Both **cauliflower** and walnuts are harvested in the **autumn**. You can eat them fresh in September. If you want to save them, though, you can. You can freeze them then **thaw** them when you are ready to eat them.

46

Words in Writing
Choose ten spelling words and two Words Across the Curriculum words. Write a sentence using each word.

1.
2.
3.
4.
5.
6.
7.
8.
9.
10.
11.
12.

Answers will vary.

Misspelled Words
Circle the correct answer in each sentence.

1. Please taste the soup before adding (**salt**, sault) or pepper.
2. After the rain, the (**lawn**, laun) was green and thick.
3. The sports hero loved to sign her (awtograph, **autograph**) for her fans.
4. The students were (**loyal**, loual) to their teacher.
5. The peridot is the birthstone for the month of (Awgust, **August**).

47

Say each of the following words out loud. Then, write each word on the lines provided.

Spelling Tip

The vowels **a**, **e**, **i**, **o**, and **u** can all be influenced by the letter **r** following them. Words with a **vowel-plus-r** spelling can make their own single-syllable sounds, with the **r** sound emphasized more than the vowel. There are many different symbols for **r**-controlled vowels: /är/ (as in *car*), /er/ (as in *fair*), /ir/ (as in *deer*), /ôr/ (as in *forest*), /ur/ (as in *urban*), and /er/ for unstressed **r**-controlled vowels.

Spelling Words

apartment	apartment
discover	discover
confirm	confirm
alligator	alligator
purple	purple
Arkansas	Arkansas
fern	fern
thirsty	thirsty
northern	northern
return	return
cougar	cougar
western	western
Virginia	Virginia
forest	forest
urban	urban

48

Words in Context
Write spelling words to complete the following paragraph. You will not use all of the words.

Challenge

Circle other **r**-controlled vowels you find in the paragraph.

Cougars

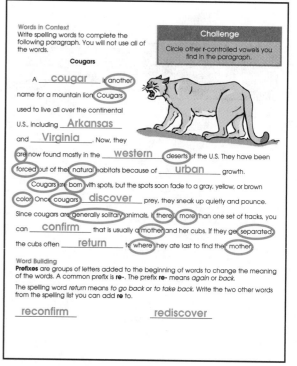

A **cougar** is (another) name for a mountain lion. (Cougars) used to live all over the continental U.S., including **Arkansas** and **Virginia**. Now, they (are) now found mostly in the **western** (deserts) of the U.S. They have been (forced) out of their (natural) habitats because of **urban** growth. (Cougars) are (born) with spots, but the spots soon fade to a gray, yellow, or brown (color). Once (cougars) **discover** prey, they sneak up quietly and pounce. Since cougars are (generally solitary) animals, if (there) are (more) than one set of tracks, you can **confirm** that is usually a (mother) and her cubs. If they get (separated), the cubs often **return** to (where) they ate last to find their (mother).

Word Building
Prefixes are groups of letters added to the beginning of words to change the meaning of the words. A common prefix is **re-**. The prefix **re-** means *again* or *back*.

The spelling word *return* means *to go back* or *to take back*. Write the two other words from the spelling list you can add **re** to.

reconfirm **rediscover**

49

Answer Key

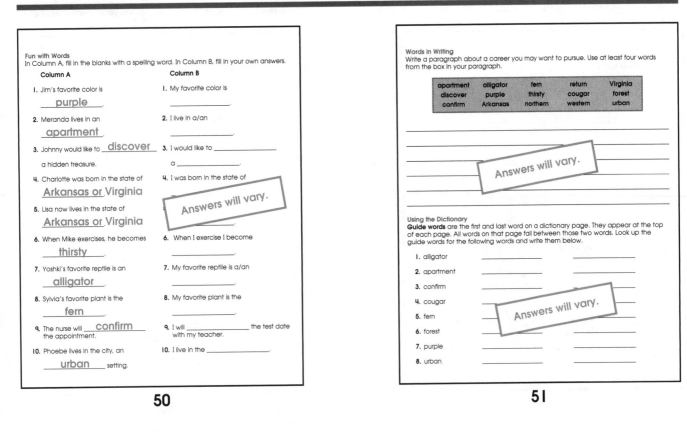

Fun with Words
In Column A, fill in the blanks with a spelling word. In Column B, fill in your own answers.

Column A	Column B
1. Jim's favorite color is purple.	1. My favorite color is ______.
2. Meranda lives in an apartment.	2. I live in a/an ______.
3. Johnny would like to discover a hidden treasure.	3. I would like to ______ a ______.
4. Charlotte was born in the state of Arkansas or Virginia	4. I was born in the state of
5. Lisa now lives in the state of Arkansas or Virginia	
6. When Mike exercises, he becomes thirsty.	6. When I exercise I become ______.
7. Yoshki's favorite reptile is an alligator.	7. My favorite reptile is a/an ______.
8. Sylvia's favorite plant is the fern.	8. My favorite plant is the ______.
9. The nurse will confirm the appointment.	9. I will ______ the test date with my teacher.
10. Phoebe lives in the city, an urban setting.	10. I live in the ______.

Answers will vary.

50

Words in Writing
Write a paragraph about a career you may want to pursue. Use at least four words from the box in your paragraph.

apartment	alligator	fern	return	Virginia
discover	purple	thirsty	cougar	forest
confirm	Arkansas	northern	western	urban

Answers will vary.

Using the Dictionary
Guide words are the first and last word on a dictionary page. They appear at the top of each page. All words on that page fall between those two words. Look up the guide words for the following words and write them below.

1. alligator
2. apartment
3. confirm
4. cougar
5. fern
6. forest
7. purple
8. urban

Answers will vary.

51

Say each word out loud. Then, write the words on the lines provided.

Spelling Tip Spelling patterns **ough** and **augh** have the same short **o** sound (found in *dog*), as the /al/, /au/, and /aw/ sounds.

Spelling Words

aught	aught
bought	bought
caught	caught
brought	brought
daughter	daughter
cough	cough
distraught	distraught
fought	fought
fraught	fraught
ought	ought
naught	naught
sought	sought
taught	taught
thought	thought
trough	trough

52

Words in Context
Complete the following poem with spelling words.

Chloe's Cough

Chloe caught a cold.
She couldn't stop her cough.
Chloe sought a cure.
She became so distraught.
Chloe ought to rest and sleep,
So her mother thought.
She brought her daughter oranges
And special teas she bought.
Finally, Chloe fought her cold
When she did just what her mother taught.

Word Building
Homophones are words that sound alike but have different spellings and meanings. Find the two spelling words that are homophones. Write the words and use a dictionary to write their definitions.

aught — anything at all

ought — to be forced by what is right or necessary

53

Answer Key

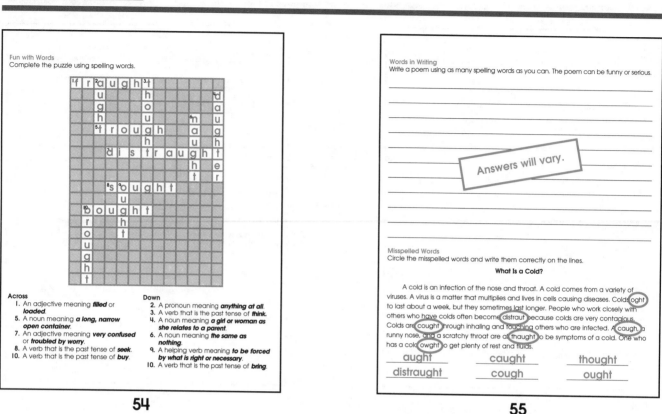

Fun with Words
Complete the puzzle using spelling words.

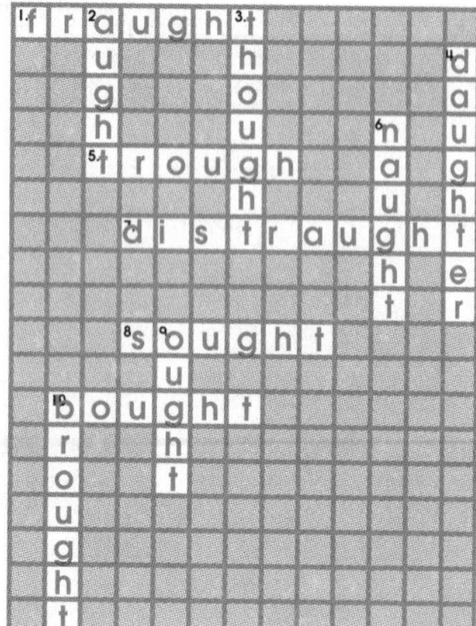

Across
1. An adjective meaning **filled** or **loaded**.
5. A noun meaning **a long, narrow open container**.
7. An adjective meaning **very confused** or **troubled by worry**.
8. A verb that is the past tense of **seek**.
10. A verb that is the past tense of **buy**.

Down
2. A pronoun meaning **anything at all**.
3. A verb that is the past tense of **think**.
4. A noun meaning **a girl or woman as she relates to a parent**.
6. A noun meaning **the same as nothing**.
9. A helping verb meaning **to be forced by what is right or necessary**.
10. A verb that is the past tense of **bring**.

54

Words in Writing
Write a poem using as many spelling words as you can. The poem can be funny or serious.

Answers will vary.

Misspelled Words
Circle the misspelled words and write them correctly on the lines.

What Is a Cold?

A cold is an infection of the nose and throat. A cold comes from a variety of viruses. A virus is a matter that multiplies and lives in cells causing diseases. Colds oght to last about a week, but they sometimes last longer. People who work closely with others who have colds often become distraut because colds are very contagious. Colds are cought through inhaling and touching others who are infected. A caugh, a runny nose, and a scratchy throat are all thaught to be symptoms of a cold. One who has a cold owght to get plenty of rest and fluids.

aught — caught — thought
distraught — cough — ought

55

Write each of the following words on the lines provided. Circle the vowel dipthongs /ou/ and /oy/. Then, underline the final /el/ vowel combination.

1. foundation — foundation
2. annoy — annoy
3. cancel — cancel
4. our — our
5. loyal — loyal
6. label — label

Write each of the following spelling words on the lines. Circle the letters that make the short **o** sound found in **dog**.

1. chalk — chalk
2. author — author
3. crawl — crawl
4. caught — caught
5. fought — fought
6. false — false
7. autograph — autograph
8. lawn — lawn
9. taught — taught
10. thought — thought

Complete the following sentences with words from the above list.

1. The students drew their hopscotch marks with chalk.
2. The famous author signed an autograph.
3. After the rain, we had a bright green lawn.
4. The umpire wasn't sure where the ball was caught.
5. The best friends were sorry that they fought.

56

Write each of the following spelling words on the lines. Circle the **r**-controlled vowels (including the **r**).

1. cougar — cougar
2. western — western
3. Virginia — Virginia
4. forest — forest
5. urban — urban
6. apartment — apartment
7. confirm — confirm
8. purple — purple
9. fern — fern
10. northern — northern

Complete the following paragraph with words from above.

The beautiful state of Virginia is located in the eastern part of the United States. Eastern Virginia, on the coast of the Atlantic Ocean, has many urban areas. Some Eastern Virginia cities are close to Washington, D.C. Western Virginia is mountainous. The Allegheny and Blue Ridge Mountains run through this part of Virginia. A beautiful Virginia forest is the perfect place for hiking, picnicking, and observing nature. Virginia is beautiful during all four of its amazing seasons.

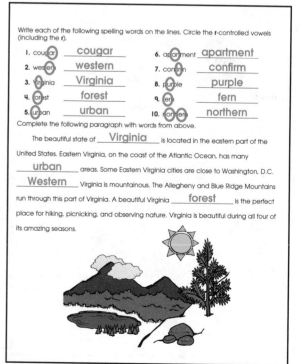

57

Answer Key

Say each of the following words out loud. Then, write each word.

Spelling Tip — **Compound words** are made by joining two words. Compound words may or may not join the meanings of the two words.

Spelling Words

applesauce	applesauce
baseball	baseball
blueprint	blueprint
bookshelf	bookshelf
cupcake	cupcake
daylight	daylight
drawbridge	drawbridge
grandparents	grandparents
haircut	haircut
horseback	horseback
housework	housework
mailbox	mailbox
sunset	sunset
textbook	textbook
volleyball	volleyball

58

Words in Context
Complete the following sentences with spelling words.

Challenge — Circle any other compound words you find.

1. Peter likes a cupake made with applesauce instead of sugar.
2. Elise's favorite activity is horseback riding on her uncle's farm.
3. When my parents finish the housework and I finish my (homework) we're going to the movies.
4. On my (birthday) the mailbox was stuffed with cards.
5. During daylight savings time, the sunset comes later in the day.
6. The architect is putting the finishing touches on the building's blueprint.
7. Dennis loves sports and plays both baseball and volleyball in school.
8. My grandparents told me about their visit to Port Clinton, where they saw a drawbridge and tall (sailboats).
9. The teacher asked Billy to put his textbook back on the bookshelf.
10. Andy's dad gets a haircut at the (barbershop) in town.

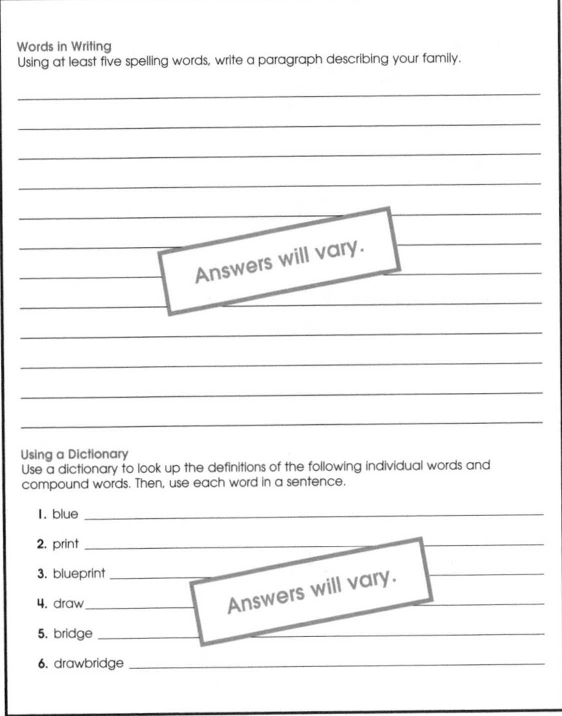

59

Fun with Words
Make new compound swords by adding a word to each word below. Use a dictionary if you need help.

1. blue + ____ = ____
2. book + ____ = ____
3. cup + ____ = ____
4. ____ = ____
5. grand + ____ = ____

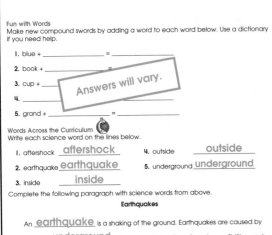

Answers will vary.

Words Across the Curriculum
Write each science word on the lines below.

1. aftershock aftershock
2. earthquake earthquake
3. inside inside
4. outside outside
5. underground underground

Complete the following paragraph with science words from above.

Earthquakes

An earthquake is a shaking of the ground. Earthquakes are caused by the shifting of underground rock or from the action of a volcano. Shifting and moving rocks cause vibrations. An aftershock can be felt toward the end of the movement of earthquakes. If you live close to an area where earthquakes are likely to occur, it is a good idea to have a safety plan. If you are outside, stay outside. If you are inside, try to get to a doorway, under a sturdy table, or by an interior wall. Knowing what to do during an earthquake is very important.

60

Words in Writing
Using at least five spelling words, write a paragraph describing your family.

Answers will vary.

Using a Dictionary
Use a dictionary to look up the definitions of the following individual words and compound words. Then, use each word in a sentence.

1. blue ____
2. print ____
3. blueprint ____
4. draw ____
5. bridge ____
6. drawbridge ____

Answers will vary.

61

Answer Key

Say each of the following contractions out loud. Then, write each word.

Spelling Tip — **Contractions** are shortened forms of words. The words are shortened by leaving out letters and replacing them with an apostrophe.

Spelling Words

I'll	I'll
I'm	I'm
she's	she's
that's	that's
they're	they're
what's	what's
you're	you're
he'd	he'd
I've	I've
we've	we've
can't	can't
don't	don't
weren't	weren't
wouldn't	wouldn't
let's	let's

62

Words in Context
The following dialogue contains words that could be written as contractions. Change the words to contractions from the spelling word list. Write them above the existing words.

(deletes letters and words) = deletes letters and words
^ = inserts words, letters, and punctuation

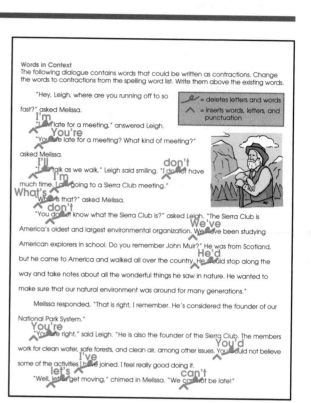

"Hey, Leigh, where are you running off to so fast?" asked Melissa.

"I am [I'm] late for a meeting," answered Leigh.

"You are [You're] late for a meeting? What kind of meeting?" asked Melissa.

"I will [I'll] talk as we walk," Leigh said smiling. "I do not [don't] have much time. I am [I'm] going to a Sierra Club meeting."

"What is [What's] that?" asked Melissa.

"You do not [don't] know what the Sierra Club is?" asked Leigh. "The Sierra Club is America's oldest and largest environmental organization. We have [We've] been studying American explorers in school. Do you remember John Muir?" He was from Scotland, but he came to America and walked all over the country. He would [He'd] stop along the way and take notes about all the wonderful things he saw in nature. He wanted to make sure that our natural environment was around for many generations."

Melissa responded, "That is right, I remember. He's considered the founder of our National Park System."

"You are [You're] right," said Leigh. "He is also the founder of the Sierra Club. The members work for clean water, safe forests, and clean air, among other issues. You would [You'd] not believe some of the activities I have [I've] joined. I feel really good doing it."

"Well, let us [let's] get moving," chimed in Melissa. "We cannot [can't] be late!"

63

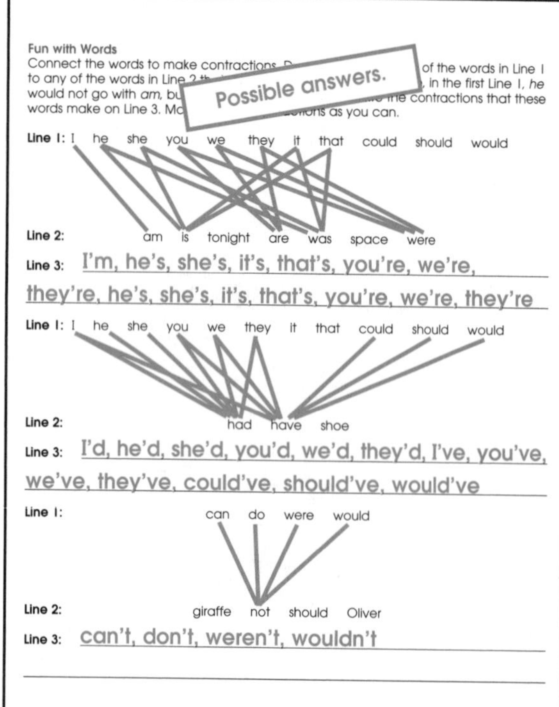

Fun with Words
Connect the words to make contractions. D... of the words in Line 1 to any of the words in Line 2 ... in the first Line 1, *he* would not go with *am*, bu... the contractions that these words make on Line 3. Mo... as you can.

Possible answers.

Line 1: I he she you we they it that could should would
Line 2: am is tonight are was space were
Line 3: I'm, he's, she's, it's, that's, you're, we're, they're, he's, she's, it's, that's, you're, we're, they're

Line 1: I he she you we they it that could should would
Line 2: had have shoe
Line 3: I'd, he'd, she'd, you'd, we'd, they'd, I've, you've, we've, they've, could've, should've, would've

Line 1: can do were would
Line 2: giraffe not should Oliver
Line 3: can't, don't, weren't, wouldn't

64

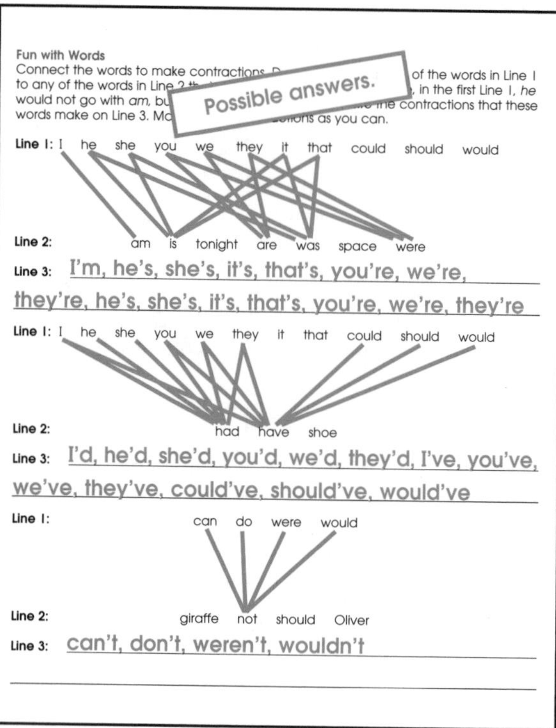

Fun with Words
Connect the words to make contractions. D... of the words in Line 1 to any of the words in Line 2 ... in the first Line 1, *he* would not go with *am*, bu... the contractions that these words make on Line 3. Mo... as you can.

Possible answers.

Line 1: I he she you we they it that could should would
Line 2: am is tonight are was space were
Line 3: I'm, he's, she's, it's, that's, you're, we're, they're, he's, she's, it's, that's, you're, we're, they're

Line 1: I he she you we they it that could should would
Line 2: had have shoe
Line 3: I'd, he'd, she'd, you'd, we'd, they'd, I've, you've, we've, they've, could've, should've, would've

Line 1: can do were would
Line 2: giraffe not should Oliver
Line 3: can't, don't, weren't, wouldn't

65

Answer Key

Write each of the following spelling words. Circle the two individual words that make up the compound words. Circle the apostrophes in the contractions.

1. applesauce — applesauce
2. I'm — I'm
3. blueprint — blueprint
4. that's — that's
5. cupcake — cupcake
6. what's — what's
7. drawbridge — drawbridge
8. he'd — he'd
9. haircut — haircut
10. we've — we've
11. housework — housework
12. don't — don't
13. sunset — sunset
14. wouldn't — wouldn't
15. volleyball — volleyball
16. I'll — I'll
17. textbook — textbook
18. let's — let's
19. baseball — baseball
20. she's — she's

66

Below is a blueprint for a house where some Olympic athletes will live. Most of the places are labeled, but four outside areas are not. Choose words from Word Box A to label the unlabeled outside areas.

Word Box A: baseball, bookshelf, daylight, drawbridge, grandparents, housework, mailbox, sunset, volleyball

BED RM. 1, BATH 1, PATIO, KITCHEN, BED RM. 2, LIVING RM., BATH 2, BED RM. 3, ENTRY, PORCH

volleyball
baseball
mailbox
drawbridge

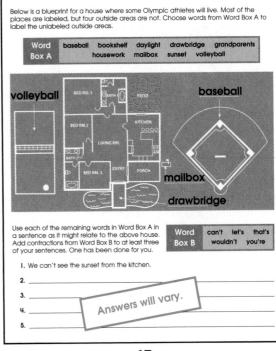

Use each of the remaining words in Word Box A in a sentence as it might relate to the above house. Add contractions from Word Box B to at least three of your sentences. One has been done for you.

Word Box B: can't, let's, that's, wouldn't, you're

1. We can't see the sunset from the kitchen.
2.
3.
4.
5.

Answers will vary.

67

Say each of the following plural nouns out loud. Then, write each word.

Spelling Tip

Following are the rules for making nouns plural:
Most nouns are made plural by adding **s** to the singular form.
Nouns ending in **s**, **x**, **z**, **ch**, and **sh** are made by adding **es**.
Nouns ending in **y** with a vowel before the **y** are formed by adding an **s**.
Nouns ending in **y** with a consonant before the **y** are formed by changing the **y** to **i** and add **es**.
Nouns ending in **o** with a vowel before the **o** are formed by adding **s**.
Nouns ending in **o** with a consonant before the **o** are formed by adding **es**.

Spelling Words

friends	friends
passes	passes
taxes	taxes
buzzes	buzzes
benches	benches
bushes	bushes
donkeys	donkeys
batteries	batteries
patios	patios
echoes	echoes
pictures	pictures
valleys	valleys
centuries	centuries
radios	radios
tomatoes	tomatoes

68

Words in Context
Complete the following narrative with spelling words. Not all of the words will be used.

Challenge
Find other regular plural words in the narrative and circle them.

Mary, Jim, Robyn, Peter, Christina, and Robert were best **friends**. They had known each other since first grade. On the last day of fifth grade, they sat on some **benches**, talking about the last year.

"Remember the time Robert crashed his model airplane into the **bushes**, and we all searched and searched for (hours)," asked Robyn. "It seemed like it took **centuries** to find, but we ended up having a blast."

"How about the time we all tried making spaghetti in Mary's mom's kitchen?" said Jim. "We had crushed **tomatoes** all over everything!"

"I'm really going to miss Mrs. Bell in science class. She didn't even mind when we set up all of those **radios** to try to break the sound barrier," said Peter.

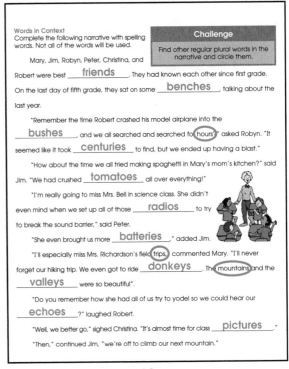

"She even brought us more **batteries**," added Jim.

"I'll especially miss Mrs. Richardson's field (trips)," commented Mary. "I'll never forget our hiking trip. We even got to ride **donkeys**. The (mountains) and the **valleys** were so beautiful".

"Do you remember how she had all of us try to yodel so we could hear our **echoes**?" laughed Robert.

"Well, we better go," sighed Christina. "It's almost time for class **pictures**."

"Then," continued Jim, "we're off to climb our next mountain."

69

Answer Key

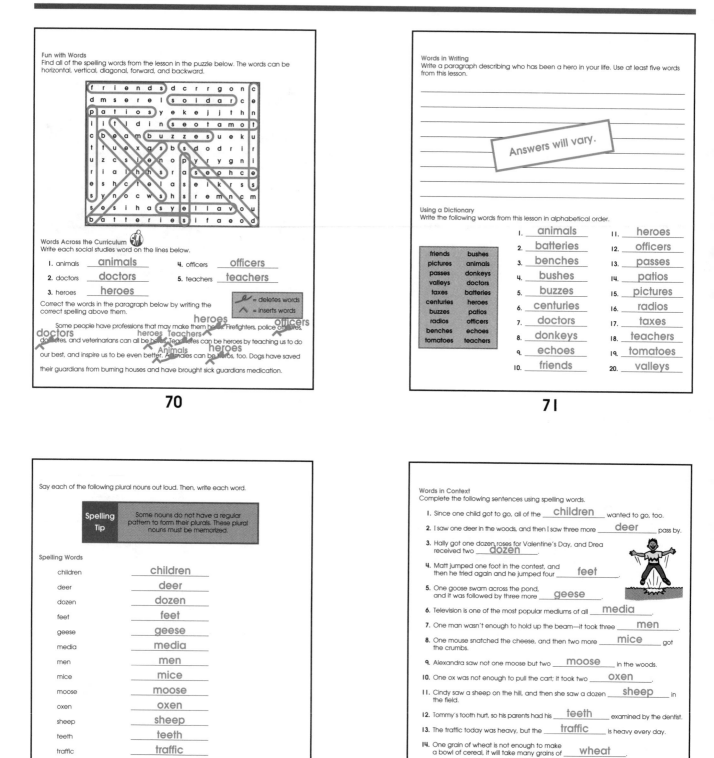

Fun with Words

Find all of the spelling words from the lesson in the puzzle below. The words can be horizontal, vertical, diagonal, forward, and backward.

f	r	i	e	n	d	s	d	c	r	r	g	o	n	c
d	m	s	e	r	e	l	s	o	i	d	a	r	c	e
p	a	t	i	o	s	y	e	k	e	j	j	t	h	n
i	i	t	l	d	i	n	s	e	o	t	a	m	o	t
c	b	e	a	m	b	u	z	z	e	s	u	e	k	u
t	t	u	e	x	g	s	b	s	d	o	d	r	i	r
u	z	c	s	i	e	n	o	p	y	r	y	g	n	i
r	i	a	l	h	h	s	r	a	s	e	o	h	c	e
e	s	h	c	t	e	l	a	s	e	i	k	r	s	s
s	y	n	o	c	w	s	h	s	r	e	m	n	c	m
s	e	s	i	h	a	s	y	e	l	l	a	v	o	u
b	a	t	t	e	r	i	e	s	i	f	a	e	o	d

Words Across the Curriculum

Write each social studies word on the lines below.

1. animals animals
2. doctors doctors
3. heroes heroes
4. officers officers
5. teachers teachers

Correct the words in the paragraph below by writing the correct spelling above them.

(deletes words) = deletes words
^ = inserts words

Some people have professions that may make them ~~heros~~ heroes. Firefighters, police ~~offiseres~~ officers, ~~doctores~~ doctors, and veterinarians can all be ~~heros~~ heroes. ~~Teacheres~~ Teachers can be heroes by teaching us to do our best, and inspire us to be even better. ~~Animales~~ Animals can be ~~heros~~ heroes, too. Dogs have saved their guardians from burning houses and have brought sick guardians medication.

70

Words in Writing

Write a paragraph describing who has been a hero in your life. Use at least five words from this lesson.

Answers will vary.

Using a Dictionary

Write the following words from this lesson in alphabetical order.

friends	bushes
pictures	animals
passes	donkeys
valleys	doctors
taxes	batteries
centuries	heroes
buzzes	patios
radios	officers
benches	echoes
tomatoes	teachers

1. animals
2. batteries
3. benches
4. bushes
5. buzzes
6. centuries
7. doctors
8. donkeys
9. echoes
10. friends
11. heroes
12. officers
13. passes
14. patios
15. pictures
16. radios
17. taxes
18. teachers
19. tomatoes
20. valleys

71

Say each of the following plural nouns out loud. Then, write each word.

Spelling Tip Some nouns do not have a regular pattern to form their plurals. These plural nouns must be memorized.

Spelling Words

children	children
deer	deer
dozen	dozen
feet	feet
geese	geese
media	media
men	men
mice	mice
moose	moose
oxen	oxen
sheep	sheep
teeth	teeth
traffic	traffic
wheat	wheat
women	women

72

Words in Context

Complete the following sentences using spelling words.

1. Since one child got to go, all of the children wanted to go, too.
2. I saw one deer in the woods, and then I saw three more deer pass by.
3. Hally got one dozen roses for Valentine's Day, and Drea received two dozen.
4. Matt jumped one foot in the contest, and then he tried again and he jumped four feet.
5. One goose swam across the pond, and it was followed by three more geese.
6. Television is one of the most popular mediums of all media.
7. One man wasn't enough to hold up the beam—it took three men.
8. One mouse snatched the cheese, and then two more mice got the crumbs.
9. Alexandra saw not one moose but two moose in the woods.
10. One ox was not enough to pull the cart; it took two oxen.
11. Cindy saw a sheep on the hill, and then she saw a dozen sheep in the field.
12. Tommy's tooth hurt, so his parents had his teeth examined by the dentist.
13. The traffic today was heavy, but the traffic is heavy every day.
14. One grain of wheat is not enough to make a bowl of cereal, it will take many grains of wheat.
15. One woman jumped in the airport taxi, and then three more women jumped in, too.

73

Answer Key

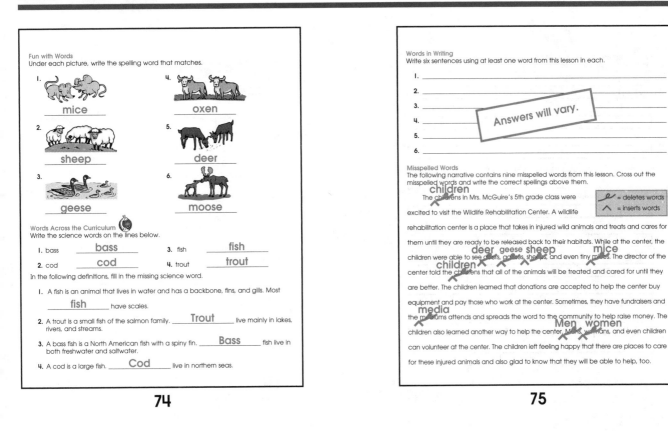

Fun with Words
Under each picture, write the spelling word that matches.

1. mice
2. sheep
3. geese
4. oxen
5. deer
6. moose

Words Across the Curriculum
Write the science words on the lines below.

1. bass — bass
2. cod — cod
3. fish — fish
4. trout — trout

In the following definitions, fill in the missing science word.

1. A fish is an animal that lives in water and has a backbone, fins, and gills. Most fish have scales.
2. A trout is a small fish of the salmon family. Trout live mainly in lakes, rivers, and streams.
3. A bass fish is a North American fish with a spiny fin. Bass fish live in both freshwater and saltwater.
4. A cod is a large fish. Cod live in northern seas.

74

Words in Writing
Write six sentences using at least one word from this lesson in each.

1. ______
2. ______
3. ______
4. ______
5. ______
6. ______

Answers will vary.

Misspelled Words
The following narrative contains nine misspelled words from this lesson. Cross out the misspelled words and write the correct spellings above them.

(deletes words) = deletes words
^ = inserts words

The ~~childrens~~ children in Mrs. McGuire's 5th grade class were excited to visit the Wildlife Rehabilitation Center. A wildlife rehabilitation center is a place that takes in injured wild animals and treats and cares for them until they are ready to be released back to their habitats. While at the center, the children were able to see ~~deers~~ deer, ~~gooses~~ geese, ~~sheeps~~ sheep, and even tiny ~~mices~~ mice. The director of the center told the ~~childrens~~ children that all of the animals will be treated and cared for until they are better. The children learned that donations are accepted to help the center buy equipment and pay those who work at the center. Sometimes, they have fundraisers and the ~~mediums~~ media attends and spreads the word to the community to help raise money. The children also learned another way to help the center. ~~Mans~~ Men, ~~womans~~ women, and even children can volunteer at the center. The children left feeling happy that there are places to care for these injured animals and also glad to know that they will be able to help, too.

75

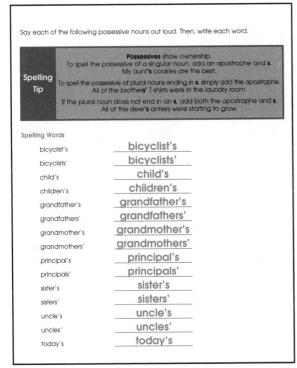

Say each of the following possessive nouns out loud. Then, write each word.

Spelling Tip

Possessives show ownership.
To spell the possessive of a singular noun, add an apostrophe and **s**.
My aunt**'s** cookies are the best.
To spell the possessive of plural nouns ending in **s**, simply add the apostrophe.
All of the brothers**'** T-shirts were in the laundry room.
If the plural noun does not end in an **s**, add both the apostrophe and **s**.
All of the deer**'s** antlers were starting to grow.

Spelling Words

bicyclist's	bicyclist's
bicyclists'	bicyclists'
child's	child's
children's	children's
grandfather's	grandfather's
grandfathers'	grandfathers'
grandmother's	grandmother's
grandmothers'	grandmothers'
principal's	principal's
principals'	principals'
sister's	sister's
sisters'	sisters'
uncle's	uncle's
uncles'	uncles'
today's	today's

76

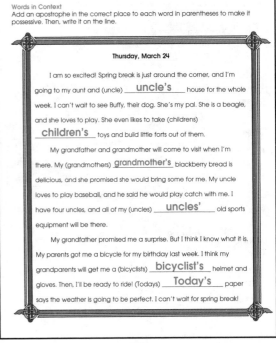

Words in Context
Add an apostrophe in the correct place to each word in parentheses to make it possessive. Then, write it on the line.

Thursday, March 24

I am so excited! Spring break is just around the corner, and I'm going to my aunt and (uncle) uncle's house for the whole week. I can't wait to see Buffy, their dog. She's my pal. She is a beagle, and she loves to play. She even likes to take (childrens) children's toys and build little forts out of them.

My grandfather and grandmother will come to visit when I'm there. My (grandmothers) grandmother's blackberry bread is delicious, and she promised she would bring some for me. My uncle loves to play baseball, and he said he would play catch with me. I have four uncles, and all of my (uncles) uncles' old sports equipment will be there.

My grandfather promised me a surprise. But I think I know what it is. My parents got me a bicycle for my birthday last week. I think my grandparents will get me a (bicyclists) bicyclist's helmet and gloves. Then, I'll be ready to ride! (Todays) Today's paper says the weather is going to be perfect. I can't wait for spring break!

77

Answer Key

Fun with Words
Choose a spelling word that belongs in each sentence and fits in the boxes. Write the words in the boxes. Apostrophes get their own box.

1. My ______________ office is on the first floor of the school.
p r i n c i p a l ' s
2. The ______________ coloring book was in his backpack.
c h i l d ' s
3. Last night's sports scores are in ______________ newspaper.
t o d a y ' s
4. All of the ______________ helmets were the same style.
b i c y c l i s t s '
5. Emma liked to borrow her oldest ______________ clothes.
s i s t e r ' s
6. All of my aunt and ______________ houses are in Arizona.
u n c l e s '
7. My grandfather and ______________ recipes are from their ancestors. or uncle's
g r a n d m o t h e r ' s
8. The ______________ jersey got muddy from the puddles.
b i c y c l i s t ' s
9. The ______________ toys were in the play box.
c h i l d r e n ' s
10. All of the bride's brothers' vests and ______________ dresses were ready.
s i s t e r s '

78

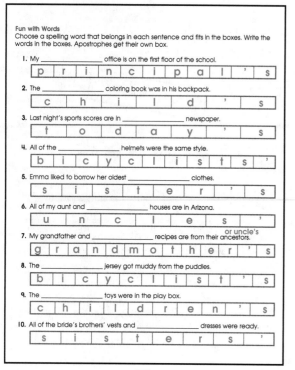

Words in Writing
Write a journal entry about something you have done recently. Use at least five possessive words in your entry.

Answers will vary.

Using a Dictionary
Write the definition of each spelling word below. Then, use each word in a sentence.

1. bicyclist's
2. bicyclists'
3. child's
4. children's
5. grandfather's
6. grandfathers'

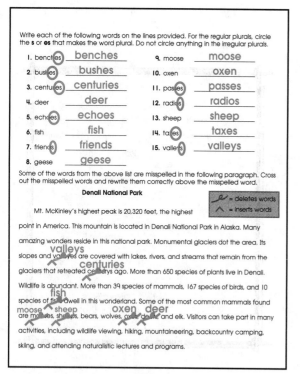

Answers will vary.

79

Write each of the following words on the lines provided. For the regular plurals, circle the **s** or **es** that makes the word plural. Do not circle anything in the irregular plurals.

1. benches — benches
2. bushes — bushes
3. centuries — centuries
4. deer — deer
5. echoes — echoes
6. fish — fish
7. friends — friends
8. geese — geese
9. moose — moose
10. oxen — oxen
11. passes — passes
12. radios — radios
13. sheep — sheep
14. taxes — taxes
15. valleys — valleys

Some of the words from the above list are misspelled in the following paragraph. Cross out the misspelled words and rewrite them correctly above the misspelled word.

Denali National Park

(deletes words / ^ = inserts words)

Mt. McKinley's highest peak is 20,320 feet, the highest point in America. This mountain is located in Denali National Park in Alaska. Many amazing wonders reside in this national park. Monumental glaciers dot the area. Its slopes and ~~valyes~~ valleys are covered with lakes, rivers, and streams that remain from the glaciers that retreated ~~centurys~~ centuries ago. More than 650 species of plants live in Denali. Wildlife is abundant. More than 39 species of mammals, 167 species of birds, and 10 species of ~~fishs~~ fish dwell in this wonderland. Some of the most common mammals found are ~~mooses~~ moose, ~~sheeps~~ sheep, bears, wolves, ~~oxes~~ oxen, ~~deers~~ deer, and elk. Visitors can take part in many activities, including wildlife viewing, hiking, mountaineering, backcountry camping, skiing, and attending naturalistic lectures and programs.

80

Write each of the following words on the lines provided. Circle the apostrophe or the apostrophe and **s** that make the words possessive.

1. bicyclists' — bicyclists'
2. child's — child's
3. children's — children's
4. grandfathers' — grandfathers'
5. principal's — principal's
6. sisters' — sisters'
7. uncle's — uncle's
8. today's — today's

The words in the above list are scrambled in the following sentences. Unscramble and write them on the lines following each sentence.

1. The teacher asked her students to write ytoda's date on their papers. — today's
2. All of the sr'siste pictures were in the yearbook. — sisters' or sister's
3. The csh'inledr books were on the lower shelf. — children's
4. My clneu's classic car is a beautiful matte yellow. — uncle's
5. The main nplr'scpial goal was the education and well being of her students. — principal's
6. My rnftes'gadahr umbrella was in the hall closet, next to his coat. — grandfathers'
7. The clybl'tsisc bags were filled with water, bananas, bagels, and power bars for her bike ride later that day. — bicyclist's
8. Brook's daughter ordered the lc'hids meal. — child's

81

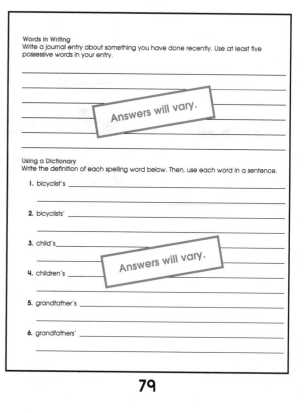

Answer Key

Say each of the following words out loud. Then, write each word.

Spelling Tip A **prefix** is a group of letters that is added to the beginning of a base word to change its meaning. The prefix **dis-** means *opposite*. The prefix **pre-** means *before*. The prefix **un-** means *not*.

Spelling Words

disappoint	disappoint
prepaid	prepaid
unable	unable
disapprove	disapprove
prerecorded	prerecorded
unbeaten	unbeaten
discover	discover
preset	preset
unhappy	unhappy
dishonest	dishonest
preschool	preschool
unlimited	unlimited
disorder	disorder
pretest	pretest
unsure	unsure

82

Words in Context
Complete the following narrative by filling in the blanks with spelling words. You may use some words more than once.

The room was in disorder. Alicia didn't want to disappoint her parents. But how was she going to clean up this mess before her parents got home from picking up her brother at preschool? At first, Alicia's parents had said, "We disapprove of you having a puppy right now." They thought she would be unable to take care of a puppy and keep up with her studies. She understood how important it was to care for a pet. Her parents showed an unlimited amount of patience and understanding, and she was eventually allowed to get one.

Alicia was running late for volleyball practice when she left that morning. Now, she had to find her textbook to study for a pretest. "If my parents discover I've let things go, they'll never trust me again," Alicia said to her new puppy, Buzz. Buzz scampered over to her desk, pulled off an envelope, and brought it to Alicia. "I forgot, I got this from the animal shelter. It's a flyer for puppy training classes and a prepaid envelope. I was unsure about taking you to training, but you may be right," she said.

Alicia heard her parents pull up in the driveway. "Well, they may be unhappy about my room, but I think they will be happy with our decision!"

83

Fun with Words
Solve the following rhymes with a spelling word.

1. Tana was so happy; she just passed the test.
   Alex was not happy; he did not do his best.
   Alex was unhappy.
2. Donald had to pay the bill as it was overdue.
   Richard's bill was paid before by his friend Drew.
   Richard's bill was prepaid.
3. Courtney was able to stay on top and make the gymnastics team.
   Vanessa did well on the bars but was not able to stay on the beam.
   Vanessa was unable to stay on the beam.

Words Across the Curriculum
Write the history words on the lines.

1. disagree disagree
2. dispute dispute
3. preamble preamble

Choose words from the list above to complete the following paragraph.

The U.S. Constitution is a document in which the laws and rules of the United States are recorded. The U.S. Constitution was drawn up and signed in 1787. The constitution consists of seven articles, a preamble that comes before the constitution and explains its purpose, and 27 amendments have been added afterward. Some people have found the wording of the U.S. Constitution to be unclear and open to interpretation. A dispute existed over the power between the union and states rights. To this day, some people disagree about the meaning of the U.S. Constitution.

84

Words in Writing
Write a short, descriptive narrative with at least two characters. Use at least five words from this lesson in your narrative. You can also use other words with the prefixes **dis-**, **pre-**, or **un-**.

Answers will vary.

Misspelled Words
The prefixes in Column A are all mixed up. Rewrite the words in Column B with the correct prefixes.

Column A	Column B
1. unhonest	dishonest
2. disrecorded	prerecorded
3. disbeaten	unbeaten
4. precover	discover
5. disset	preset
6. dislimited	unlimited

85

Answer Key

Say each of the following words out loud. Then, write each word.

Spelling Tip A **suffix** is a group of letters that are added to the end of a base word to change its meaning. The suffixes **-ion**, **-tion**, and **-ation** mean *the state or quality of.*

Spelling Words

ambition	ambition
instruction	instruction
admiration	admiration
champion	champion
interception	interception
appreciation	appreciation
companion	companion
production	production
education	education
conclusion	conclusion
rejection	rejection
imagination	imagination
possession	possession
tradition	tradition
preparation	preparation

86

Words in Context
Some of the spelling words are scrambled in the following biography. Unscramble the words and rewrite them above the scrambled words.

Mikhail Baryshnikov

It takes talent and a lot of practice. It takes bmntiaoi (ambition) and gamtaininio (imagination). It also takes some luck. Becoming a famous dancer is not easy. One of the world's most famous dancers is Mikhail Baryshnikov. Born in Russia in 1948, Baryshnikov danced with the Kirov Ballet in Russia until 1974. He was highly respected and held the tmraidoani (admiration) of the Russian people. He defected to America in 1974 and joined the American Ballet Theatre and the New York City Ballet. He has performed and choreographed many ballets. He won the prcainapeito (appreciation) of the American audiences through his work in theatre, movies, and television. Baryshnikov also tours with his own modern dance poutonicdr (production) company. The Baryshnikov Dance Foundation supports new and mid-career dancers, musicians, and other artists in training and developing their crafts. Baryshnikov's intense niaaepotrrp (preparation) for his art and his powerful and graceful performances have brought him a life long career and devoted audiences.

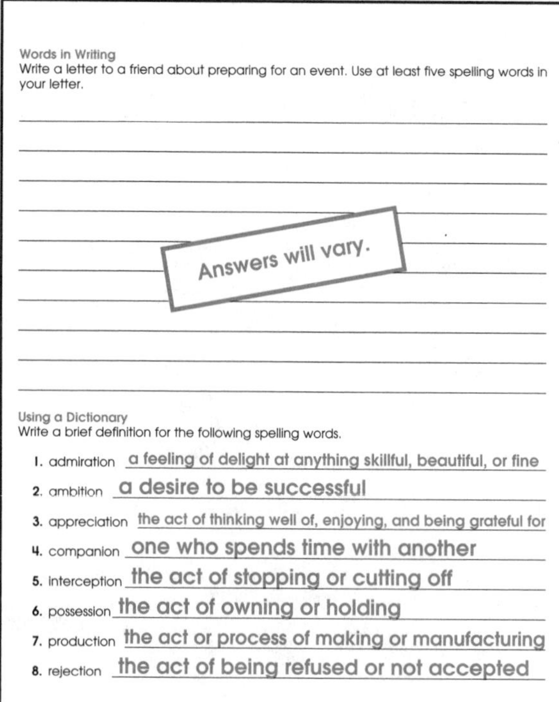

87

Fun with Words
Choose a spelling word that completes each sentence.

1. The football team was the champion of the state.
2. It is a popular tradition to eat pumpkin pie on Thanksgiving.
3. The man needed better instruction on how to assemble the bookcase.
4. Sarah's photograph of her family was her most prized possession.
5. Kelly's dog, Abby, was her constant companion and best friend.
6. The author was sad over the rejection of his book but hopeful that the next one would be accepted.
7. The interception led to a victory for the team.
8. The book had a twist near the end, and Vicki was surprised by the book's conclusion.

Words Across the Curriculum
Write the social studies words on the lines.

1. deflation deflation
2. depression depression
3. inflation inflation
4. recession recession

Complete the following paragraph with words from above.

Economics

Have you ever heard the word *inflation?* Inflation means a large rise in the price of goods and services. What would be the opposite of inflation? deflation means the prices of goods and services are falling. You have probably read or heard about the Great Depression. You've probably also heard the word *recession.* A recession is a mild depression. These are all terms that explain how the economy works.

88

Words in Writing
Write a letter to a friend about preparing for an event. Use at least five spelling words in your letter.

Answers will vary.

Using a Dictionary
Write a brief definition for the following spelling words.

1. admiration a feeling of delight at anything skillful, beautiful, or fine
2. ambition a desire to be successful
3. appreciation the act of thinking well of, enjoying, and being grateful for
4. companion one who spends time with another
5. interception the act of stopping or cutting off
6. possession the act of owning or holding
7. production the act or process of making or manufacturing
8. rejection the act of being refused or not accepted

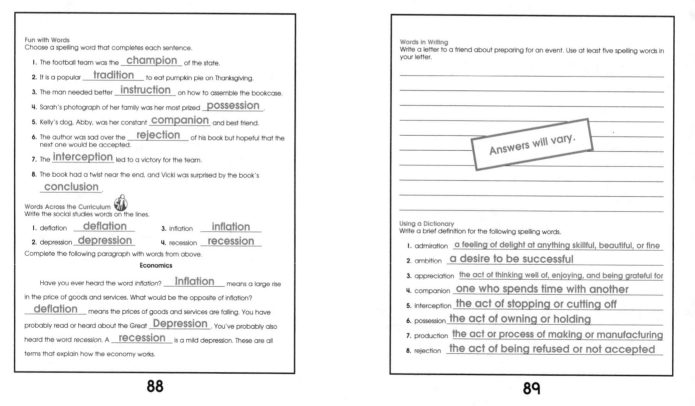

89

Answer Key

Write each of the following spelling words on the lines. Circle the prefixes.

1. (dis)approve disapprove
2. (pre)paid prepaid
3. (un)limited unlimited
4. (dis)order disorder
5. (pre)set preset
6. (un)sure unsure

Use a dictionary to define the base words and whole words and use them in sentences.

1. definition of base word: ______
   definition of word with prefix: ______
   sentence: ______
2. definition of base word: ______
   definition of word with prefix: ______
   sentence: ______
3. definition of base word: ______
   definition of word with prefix: ______
   sentence: ______
4. definition of base word: ______
   definition of word with prefix: ______
   sentence: ______
5. definition of base word: ______
   definition of word with prefix: ______
   sentence: ______
6. definition of base word: ______
   definition of word with prefix: ______
   sentence: ______

Answers will vary.

90

Write each of the following spelling words on the lines. Circle the suffixes.

1. conclu(sion) conclusion
2. posses(sion) possession
3. instruc(tion) instruction
4. intercep(tion) interception
5. produc(tion) production
6. rejec(tion) rejection
7. admir(ation) admiration
8. appreci(ation) appreciation
9. imagin(ation) imagination
10. prepar(ation) preparation

Complete the following sentences using words from the above list.

1. If the mountain hikers are well prepared, then they have spent much time in preparation.
2. If the students like to pretend, then they have an active imagination.
3. If the teacher's efforts are appreciated, then the teacher has received appreciation.
4. If people admire the artists, then the artists have received admiration.
5. If the application is denied, then the one who has applied has received a rejection.
6. If the farmer grows many tomatoes, then his production of tomatoes is large.
7. If the football player is in position to intercept the ball, then there is a good chance the play will result in an interception.
8. If the teacher instructs, then what he teaches is his instruction.
9. If one possesses something, the thing one owns is his or her possession.
10. If the speaker concludes his speech with a joke, then the joke is the conclusion.

91

Say each of the following words out loud. Then, write each word on the lines.

Spelling Tip: **Rhyming words** are words that have the same sounds at the ends of the word. Even though the spellings may be different, rhymes are made from the same vowel sounds.

Spelling Words

Spelling Words	
apple	apple
dapple	dapple
center	center
enter	enter
prince	prince
mince	mince
clock	clock
stock	stock
bake	bake
cake	cake
city	city
ditty	ditty
flute	flute
fruit	fruit
hoot	hoot

92

Fun with Words

Circle all of the spelling words you find in this story. Write the words you circled on the lines below. Underline other pairs of rhyming words that are not spelling words.

This little ditty is about a prince
A young prince named Prince Vitty.
Prince Vitty lived in a kingdom,
A kingdom within a big city.
Prince Vitty had some favorite things.
Prince Vitty loved a good apple.
He was lucky that his field
Had a bunches of apples.
Prince Vitty also liked to play.
He played a lovely flute.
In his fields, he'd play and hoot
And eat lots of shiny fruit.
Prince Vitty had another love.
Prince Vitty liked to bake.
What do you think his favorite was?
Why it was dapple apple cake.
Prince Vitty was a good baker.
And Prince Vitty played the flute well.
It's too bad he had a job
That made him want to yell.
Prince Vitty couldn't stay outside
He had to watch his clock.
He had to get back to his job,
Which was to watch the stock.
He really didn't like his job,
Which had to do with money.
He would rather play his flute
And sit by a lake that's sunny.
It's not that the prince didn't like to work.
He wanted to earn his keep.
He just had his own ideas
On the rewards he wanted to reap.
One day, his father saw the prince
Return from the lake to enter
The business place of the kingdom
Where stocks and bonds were the center.
Poor Prince Vitty looked so sad,
With thoughts of music and cake
His father Vince could no longer stand
To continue his terrible mistake.
"Son," his father gently said
And looked him in his eyes.
"I just want you to be happy,
So by night, mince your apples,
And by day, you can bake pies.
Prince Vitty's eyes lit up,
And he hugged his loving father.
"You know there's one who likes the stocks.
It is your only daughter."
Princess Bitty started working
With the kingdom's book
Prince Vitty gladly took the job
Of the city's only flute-playing cook.

ditty	dapple	bake	enter
prince	flute	cake	center
city	hoot	clock	mince
apple	fruit	stock	

93

Answer Key

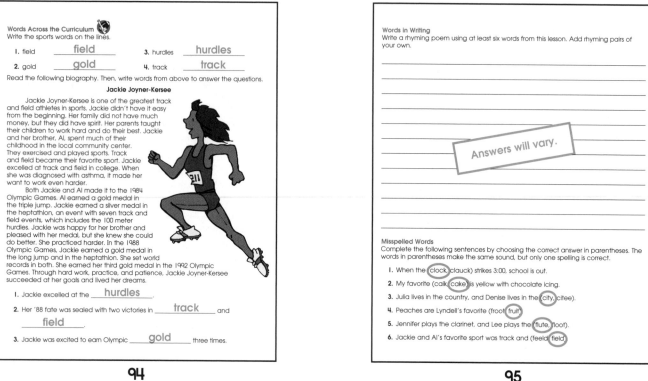

Words Across the Curriculum
Write the sports words on the lines.

1. field field
2. gold gold
3. hurdles hurdles
4. track track

Read the following biography. Then, write words from above to answer the questions.

Jackie Joyner-Kersee

Jackie Joyner-Kersee is one of the greatest track and field athletes in sports. Jackie didn't have it easy from the beginning. Her family did not have much money, but they did have spirit. Her parents taught their children to work hard and do their best. Jackie and her brother, Al, spent much of their childhood in the local community center. They exercised and played sports. Track and field became their favorite sport. Jackie excelled at track and field in college. When she was diagnosed with asthma, it made her want to work even harder.

Both Jackie and Al made it to the 1984 Olympic Games. Al earned a gold medal in the triple jump. Jackie earned a silver medal in the heptathlon, an event with seven track and field events, which includes the 100 meter hurdles. Jackie was happy for her brother and pleased with her medal, but she knew she could do better. She practiced harder. In the 1988 Olympic Games, Jackie earned a gold medal in the long jump and in the heptathlon. She set world records in both. She earned her third gold medal in the 1992 Olympic Games. Through hard work, practice, and patience, Jackie Joyner-Kersee succeeded at her goals and lived her dreams.

1. Jackie excelled at the hurdles.
2. Her '88 fate was sealed with two victories in track and field.
3. Jackie was excited to earn Olympic gold three times.

94

Words in Writing
Write a rhyming poem using at least six words from this lesson. Add rhyming pairs of your own.

Answers will vary.

Misspelled Words
Complete the following sentences by choosing the correct answer in parentheses. The words in parentheses make the same sound, but only one spelling is correct.

1. When the (clock, clauck) strikes 3:00, school is out. [clock]
2. My favorite (caik, cake) is yellow with chocolate icing. [cake]
3. Julia lives in the country, and Denise lives in the (city, citee). [city]
4. Peaches are Lyndell's favorite (froot, fruit). [fruit]
5. Jennifer plays the clarinet, and Lee plays the (flute, floot). [flute]
6. Jackie and Al's favorite sport was track and (feeld, field). [field]

95

Say each of the following words out loud. Then, write each word on the lines provided.

Spelling Tip — **Homophones** are words that sound the same but are spelled differently and have different meanings.

Spelling Words

ate	ate
eight	eight
beach	beach
beech	beech
board	board
bored	bored
feat	feat
feet	feet
serf	serf
surf	surf
waist	waist
waste	waste
pair	pair
pare	pare
pear	pear

96

Words in Context
Complete the following sentences with spelling words. Use a dictionary if you need help.

1. A beech tree has dark green leaves, smooth gray bark, and edible nuts.
2. A feat is an act of courage, strength, or skill.
3. In the Middle Ages, a serf was a farm worker who could be sold along with the property on which he worked.
4. A soft, yellow or green fruit that is round at one end and narrows at the other is a pear.
5. The past tense of *eat* is ate.
6. If a speaker is boring, then the audience would surely be bored.
7. The plural of the word *foot* is feet.
8. If one would pare a pear, he or she would be peeling away the rind.
9. Another word for *trash* is waste.
10. The waves of the sea breaking on the shore or reef is the surf.
11. The part of the body between the ribs and the hips is the waist.
12. A pair is a set of two.

Word Building
Write the plural form of the words below.

1. beach beaches
2. beech beeches
3. board boards
4. feat feats
5. pear pears

97

Words in Context
Read the passage and complete the sentences with spelling words.

Surfing is a fun sport where individuals ride to shore on a breaking wave. Surfers ride on surfboards. A surfer begins at the point where the wave begins to form. Then, the surfer starts paddling toward the beach with the oncoming wave. The surfer stands up when the wave catches the board. The surfer rides the crest of the wave, or if the wave is large, the tube of the wave. You have probably seen the tube in pictures with surfers riding under the overhead curl. Surfing began in Hawaii in the 19th century and spread to California in the 1920s. Hawaii remains a hotspot for surfing.

1. Surfers paddle from the beach out into the sea.
2. To be safe, it's best to surf with a pair of friends.
3. Surfing requires a lot of practice and skill. Surfing is quite a feat.

Words Across the Curriculum
Write the music words on the lines beside each word.

1. base — base
2. bass — bass
3. coarse — coarse
4. course — course

Complete the following narrative with music words.

Tim wasn't feeling well. His throat felt coarse. Music is Tim's favorite course. He has a band concert in two days. At least he plays the cymbals, so he can still practice and hopefully be well for the recital.

Tim's best friend, Theo, plays the bass in the band. Tim's favorite sport is baseball. But Theo sprained his ankle running to third base. Fortunately, it wasn't too bad, and Theo can still play with a sprained ankle. Tim and Theo's music teacher, Mr. Anton, is relieved that Tim and Theo can still play. He was starting to think it was a sign that the recital was doomed. However, both Tim and Theo recovered. The recital is a hit!

98

Words in Writing
Write a descriptive narrative using at least six words from this lesson. Make it fun and be creative!

Answers will vary.

Using a Dictionary
Hundreds of homophones exist in the English language. Use a dictionary to look up the definitions of each of these pairs of homophones. Write a brief description of each.

1. blew: past tense of *blow*
   blue: a color
2. creak: a noise
   creek: a stream
3. eyelet: a small hole for a cord to go through
   islet: a small island
4. fair: honest; a bazaar
   fare: the cost of transportation
5. hair: small growths that come from the skin
   hare: a rabbit
6. might: the past tense of *may*; strength
   mite: a small insect
7. principal: the chief
   principle: rule
8. rose: a flower
   rows: lines
9. soar: to fly
   sore: painful
10. toe: any of five parts at the end of the foot
    tow: to pull

99

Say each of the following words out loud. Then, write each word.

Spelling Tip Some words in the English language are easily confused with other, similar words. Pay careful attention to your writing to make sure you are using the correct word and spelling.

Spelling Words

adapt	adapt
adopt	adopt
accept	accept
except	except
desert	desert
dessert	dessert
of	of
off	off
weather	weather
whether	whether
were	were
where	where
breadth	breadth
breath	breath
breathe	breathe

100

Words in Context
Complete the following paragraph with spelling words. Not every word will be used. Use a dictionary if you need help.

Hiking the Grand Canyon

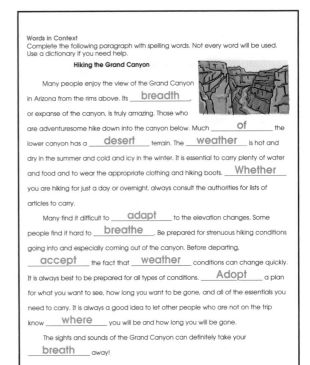

Many people enjoy the view of the Grand Canyon in Arizona from the rims above. Its breadth, or expanse of the canyon, is truly amazing. Those who are adventuresome hike down into the canyon below. Much of the lower canyon has a desert terrain. The weather is hot and dry in the summer and cold and icy in the winter. It is essential to carry plenty of water and food and to wear the appropriate clothing and hiking boots. Whether you are hiking for just a day or overnight, always consult the authorities for lists of articles to carry.

Many find it difficult to adapt to the elevation changes. Some people find it hard to breathe. Be prepared for strenuous hiking conditions going into and especially coming out of the canyon. Before departing, accept the fact that weather conditions can change quickly. It is always best to be prepared for all types of conditions. Adopt a plan for what you want to see, how long you want to be gone, and all of the essentials you need to carry. It is always a good idea to let other people who are not on the trip know where you will be and how long you will be gone.

The sights and sounds of the Grand Canyon can definitely take your breath away!

101

Fun with Words
Complete the following script with spelling words. Some words may be used more than once.

Mom: Riley and Gillian, you can have dessert after you finish your vegetables. What would you like?

Riley: I would like walnut brownies.

Gillian: I like brownies, except without nuts. Can we have lemon meringue pie?

Riley: I like lemon pie, but can you take the meringue off?

Dad: Maybe we can have something else for dessert?

Mom: Alright, how about peach cobbler for dessert, with no nuts and no meringue?

Dad: I think that is something we can all accept.

Words Across the Curriculum
Write the social studies words on the lines below.

1. emigrate emigrate
2. immigrate immigrate

Use a dictionary to define the social studies words. Then, write a sentence using each word.

1. emigrate
2. immigrate

Answers will vary.

102

Words in Writing
Create a comic strip. Write the dialogue in bubbles or in boxes of their own. Draw pictures to go along with the dialogue. Use at least six spelling words.

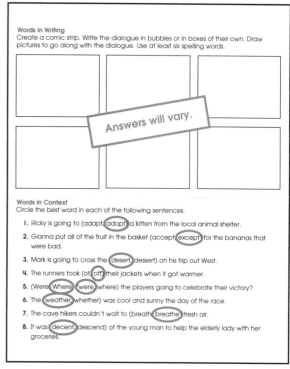

Answers will vary.

Words in Context
Circle the best word in each of the following sentences.

1. Ricky is going to (adapt, **adopt**) a kitten from the local animal shelter.
2. Gianna put all of the fruit in the basket (accept, **except**) for the bananas that were bad.
3. Mark is going to cross the (**desert**, dessert) on his trip out West.
4. The runners took (of, **off**) their jackets when it got warmer.
5. (Were, **Where**) (**were**, where) the players going to celebrate their victory?
6. The (**weather**, whether) was cool and sunny the day of the race.
7. The cave hikers couldn't wait to (breath, **breathe**) fresh air.
8. It was (**decent**, descend) of the young man to help the elderly lady with her groceries.

103

Write these words in alphabetical order. Then, look them up in the dictionary. Then, write their pronunciations, parts of speech, and definitions on the lines provided.

adventure	monkey	autograph	baseball	discover
coach	chipmunk	purple	geese	imagination

1. word: adventure
   pronunciation: ad ven' sher
   part of speech: noun
   definition: an exciting experience
2. word: autograph
   pronunciation: ôt e graf
   part of speech: noun
   definition: a signature
3. word: baseball
   pronunciation: bās' bôl
   part of speech: noun
   definition: a sport or ball used in baseball
4. word: chipmunk
   pronunciation: chip' munk
   part of speech: noun
   definition: a member of the squirrel family
5. word: coach
   pronunciation: kōch
   part of speech: noun
   definition: a trainer of athletics
6. word: discover
   pronunciation: dis skuv' er
   part of speech: verb
   definition: to find for the first time
7. word: geese
   pronunciation: gēs
   part of speech: noun
   definition: plural of goose
8. word: imagination
   pronunciation: i maj i nā shen
   part of speech: noun
   definition: a mental image
9. word: monkey
   pronunciation: mun' kē
   part of speech: noun
   definition: a primate with a long tail
10. word: purple
    pronunciation: pur' pel
    part of speech: noun
    definition: a color between red and violet

105

Write each of the following spelling words on the lines provided.

1. enter enter
2. center center
3. clock clock
4. stock stock
5. flute flute
6. fruit fruit
7. board board
8. bored bored
9. serf serf
10. surf surf
11. pare pare
12. pear pear

Complete each of the following sentences using words from above.

1. The players jumped for the ball in the center of the court.
2. The group packed nuts, cheese, bread, and fruit for their lunches.
3. The serf of the Middle Ages had a difficult life.
4. The chef used a small knife to pare the fruit.
5. The surfer was very particular about the board she used.
6. The clock on the wall seemed to tick slower and slower the closer it got to the end of the school day.

106

Write each of the following words on the lines.

1. accept accept
2. except except
3. desert desert
4. dessert dessert
5. were were
6. where where
7. breath breath
8. breathe breathe

Complete each of the following sentences using words from above.

1. Becca's class is learning about animals who live in the desert.
2. After the work out, you should breathe deeply.
3. Reggie is going to accept the invitation to the dance.
4. Where is the class going on its next field trip?
5. Strawberry shortcake is Suzie's favorite dessert.
6. After the hard work out, I almost couldn't catch my breath.
7. Dave likes all vegetables except green peppers.
8. Ricki, Lynne, and Lee were best friends.

107

Choose ten words listed from this review lesson and write them in alphabetical order. Then, use a dictionary to write the pronunciations, parts of speech, and definitions.

1. word: ______ pronunciation: ______ part of speech: ______ definition: ______
2. word: ______ pronunciation: ______ part of speech: ______ definition: ______
3. word: ______ pronunciation: ______ part of speech: ______ definition: ______
4. word: ______ pronunciation: ______ part of speech: ______ definition: ______
5. word: ______ pronunciation: ______ part of speech: ______ definition: ______
6. word: ______ pronunciation: ______ part of speech: ______ definition: ______
7. word: ______ pronunciation: ______ part of speech: ______ definition: ______
8. word: ______ pronunciation: ______ part of speech: ______ definition: ______
9. word: ______ pronunciation: ______ part of speech: ______ definition: ______
10. word: ______ pronunciation: ______ part of speech: ______ definition: ______

Answers will vary.

108

Choose ten words of your own and write them in alphabetical order. Then, use a dictionary to write the pronunciations, parts of speech, and definitions.

1. word: ______ pronunciation: ______ part of speech: ______ definition: ______
2. word: ______ pronunciation: ______ part of speech: ______ definition: ______
3. word: ______ pronunciation: ______ part of speech: ______ definition: ______
4. word: ______ pronunciation: ______ part of speech: ______ definition: ______
5. word: ______ pronunciation: ______ part of speech: ______ definition: ______
6. word: ______ pronunciation: ______ part of speech: ______ definition: ______
7. word: ______ pronunciation: ______ part of speech: ______ definition: ______
8. word: ______ pronunciation: ______ part of speech: ______ definition: ______
9. word: ______ pronunciation: ______ part of speech: ______ definition: ______
10. word: ______ pronunciation: ______ part of speech: ______ definition: ______

Answers will vary.

109

Notes

Notes

Notes